Discovering Philippians/
Colossians

THE EPISTLES OF PHILIPPIANS & COLOSSIANS

Discovering Philippians/Colossians Earl F. Palmer
What This Scripture Means to Me Barbara Chafin
Photographs William S. La Sor
Book Design Elizabeth Woll
Cover Artist Ben Wolhberg

DISCOVERING PHILIPPIANS/ COLOSSIANS

The Guideposts Home Bible Study Program

GUIDEPOSTS

Carmel   New York   10512

THE GUIDEPOSTS HOME BIBLE STUDY PROGRAM
Philippians/Colossians

1. DISCOVERING PHILIPPIANS/COLOSSIANS
2. My Working Bible
3. Knowing More About Philippians/Colossians

All Scripture verses referenced herein are from the King James Version of the Bible.

Designed by Elizabeth Woll.

Printed in the United States of America.

Contents

Publisher's Introduction to Philippians   9

Preface to Philippians   11

LESSON 1   15
    What This Scripture Means to Me   28

LESSON 2   30
    What This Scripture Means to Me   43

LESSON 3   45
    What This Scripture Means to Me   58

LESSON 4   60
    What This Scripture Means to Me   71

Publisher's Introduction to Colossians   75

Preface to Colossians   77

LESSON 5   79
    What This Scripture Means to Me   90

LESSON 6   92
    What This Scripture Means to Me   102

LESSON 7   104
    What This Scripture Means to Me   114

LESSON 8   116
    What This Scripture Means to Me   127

How to Use
the Guideposts Home
Bible Study Program

Step #1. Read the passages in your *Working Bible* that are included in the appropriate lesson material in *Discovering Philippians/Colossians*. In the margins of your *Working Bible* jot down any notes you'd like to call special attention to.

Step #2. Then, to amplify the Scriptures you've read, study Lesson 1 in *Discovering Philippians/Colossians*. As you read the lesson keep your *Working Bible* open so you can look up the many Scripture references that are included in the lesson.

Step #3. When you complete each lesson, quiz yourself on what you've learned, with the quiz booklet, *Knowing More About Philippians/Colossians*.

Repeat this rhythm as you read each lesson, to get the most from your study of God's Word.

Publisher's Introduction to Philippians

Our studies bring us now to one of Paul's most personal letters with the exception of Philemon. The Christians in the church at Philippi were much loved by Paul, and they felt a strong attachment to and love for him.

Undoubtedly Paul's special feeling for his Philippian friends had its roots in the dramatic scene Luke pictured for us in Acts 16. He recounted how Paul, while on his second missionary journey, saw a vision one night in Troas—"There stood a man of Macedonia, and prayed him, saying, Come over into Macedonia, and help us."

Immediately obedient to what he felt was a call from God, Paul, along with Silas, Timothy, and Luke, engaged passage on a ship bound for Neapolis, a port on the Aegean Sea, in northeast Macedonia (now part of Greece). Upon arriving there, they traveled the ten miles inland on the Egnation Way to the important Roman city of Philippi. At Neapolis, Paul's feet touched the continent of Europe for the first time, and it was in Philippi that he first witnessed to a European audience. The year was A.D. 49.

By our standards, Philippi was an old city even at the time Paul arrived. It was founded in 358 B.C. and was named after Philip II, the father of Alexander the Great. The city was strategically located on the Via Egnatia, the primary highway that connected the Imperial city of Rome to the eastern provinces of the empire. It was here that Paul, under the guidance of the Holy Spirit, established the Christian beachhead in Europe.

Now, some fourteen or fifteen years later (A.D. 63–64), Paul writes his friends in Philippi from prison in Rome. There are several reasons why Paul wrote the letter that will become increasingly apparent in our study. He wanted to thank them for a generous gift and encourage them in the faith. The letter carries a strong appeal for unity, oneness in Christ, and warns against the false teaching of those who were corrupting the freedom message of the gospel by insisting upon certain forms of Jewish legalism.

It is in this letter that Paul has given us the magnificent Christ-hymn (Lesson 2), one of his best known and loftiest writings (2:6–11). Whether this was his own composition or quoted from another early hymn, its poetic quality and beauty have made it much loved throughout the centuries, and we are indebted to Paul for making it available to us. In it Paul lifts up Jesus Christ as *the* pattern for all Christian behavior.

Woven throughout the entire letter is a spirit of joy and encouragement as we come to an ever increasing understanding of the great and noble heart of Paul.

Preface to Philippians

Philippi was a small city in the Roman province of Macedonia. It first came to our attention in connection with Paul's second missionary journey (Acts 16). Accompanied by Silvanus (Silas), Luke, and Timothy, Paul made his first foray into Europe through this military outpost.

Upon their arrival in Philippi, the four missionary travelers first visited a place by the riverside "where prayer was wont to be made"—possibly a reference to a synagogue or, more likely, an informal place of Jewish worship. My feeling that it was informal is based on the Jewish practice that there must be ten male founders to establish a synagogue; otherwise "informal" places of prayer were set up. And Luke tells us a group of women were meeting—no mention is made of men.

The Place of Prayer.

One of the women involved in this group was Lydia, a businesswoman from the city of Thyatira. She was a Greek who had been attracted to the message of the Law and the prophets of Israel. Luke describes her as a worshiper of God. He then goes on to tell us that as Lydia heard of the fulfillment of the Old Testament hope in Jesus of Nazareth, the Lord opened her heart and "she attended unto the things which were spoken of Paul" (Acts 16:14).

This narrative of the event with the riverside Bible study

group gives us the story of the first Christian convert in Europe—a Greek woman and her family, for we read that her entire household was baptized with her. This event is most important to us because it marks the establishment of the first Christian church on the continent of Europe—the Good News of the gospel was indeed going to "all the earth."

The Healing of the Priestess of Pythus.

The next event recorded by Luke had to do with a slave girl who was apparently a priestess of Pythus. We're told she was "possessed with a spirit of divination" (Acts 16:16). And the Greek word for "divination" is the word *python* —a reference to the oracles of Delphi and the ability to foretell future events.

As the story continues, Paul sets this slave priestess free from her cultic entrapment. At this point her owners became furious because as a "future teller" she was a source of income, but now that she was healed her money-making days were over, and her owners demanded that Paul and Silas be thrown into prison as troublemakers.

Not knowing that Paul and Silas were Roman citizens, the city magistrates had them beaten and thrown into prison. An interesting sidelight is that there is no mention that Luke and Timothy were jailed—they were not Jews. Anti-Semitism was widespread throughout the first-century world. Racial discrimination and prejudice were rampant even then.

The Prison Saga.

But in prison Paul and Silas continued to share their faith "and sang praises unto God." Next Luke tells us in the Acts 16 story that some time after midnight an earthquake shook the prison and broke open the doors. The wooden beams in the common stockade collapsed and the prisoners were all freed from their bonds.

When the awakened guard saw what had happened, he immediately decided to do the honorable Roman thing— commit suicide. But Paul had persuaded the prisoners not to escape and now told the guard not to harm himself because they were all there. And it was then that the guard was introduced to the God of love as he asked, "Sirs, what must I do to be saved?" (Acts 16:30).

A Growing Church.

With these beginnings, the church at Philippi grew. It

was quite natural for this fledgling congregation to become strongly attached to Paul, their father in the Lord. They cared for him and over the years gave him both emotional and physical support. Also, this spirit of love and caring could be seen in the way they contributed to the needs of the Jerusalem Christians who were suffering from famine and persecution (2 Cor. 8:1–7).

This brief review of the beginnings of the Philippian church helps us to appreciate something of its atmosphere. I'm sure their strong interest in Paul caused them to follow all his journeys and activities closely. They would have known about his efforts in Corinth and Ephesus and about his visit to Jerusalem.

The Mood of the Church at Philippi.

But they were undoubtedly out of touch with him during his house arrest in Caesarea (Acts 23:31–26:30) and during his long sea journey to Rome (Acts 27–28). Now, however, contact was reestablished and they learned of his arrest and that he was awaiting trial before Emperor Nero.

Nero ruled as Emperor from A.D. 54 through 68. During his younger years he was content to allow the pragmatic Afrianius Burrus and the wise Lucius Annaeus Seneca to administer the affairs of the office of the Emperor. These were relatively moderate years because of the evenhanded policies of Burrus and Seneca. An example of this sense of fairness is seen in Acts 18 as Paul stands before Seneca's brother Gallio, who is Prefect of the province of Achaia. In this episode Gallio supports the right to free religious expression and refuses to interfere with Paul's right to teach the gospel in Corinth.

The Mood in Rome.

But by the time Paul arrived in Rome as a prisoner, a dark cloud was forming over the Empire and moral deterioration was taking form in the institution of the Emperor. Nero would arrange for the murder of Burrus and Seneca in A.D. 65, and he would personally preside over a reign of chaotic brutality unmatched in the history of any great city.

Before his death, Seneca referred to his beloved city of Rome as a "sewer" of decadence and lust. It was on the eve of these terrible days that Paul arrived in the Imperial City.

Undoubtedly the Philippian Christians were aware of what was happening in Rome, and out of concern for Paul they sent one of their young church members, named Epaphroditus, to serve and be of help to him. This was not all that different from what goes on with prisoners in certain parts of our world today—to survive, they need friends on the outside to supply them with food and essential goods.

But after a time, Epaphroditus became ill, and Paul decided that he should send his young friend and helper home (Phil. 2:26). He also decided to send Timothy with Epaphroditus, and the two of them carried this letter to Philippi.

It is likely this letter is one of Paul's last. And now, we who live almost 2,000 years later are the beneficiaries of that young man who became ill in Rome and his wise friend who had the good sense to send him home. Because of these events, we have the priceless gift of this letter of Paul to his beloved Christian friends in Philippi.

LESSON 1
PHILIPPIANS 1

Courageous Faith

Dear Lord, Help me to understand this lesson and apply its truths to my life. AMEN.

In this letter, Paul follows the tradition of first-century Greek letter writing by identifying himself right at the beginning (1:1–2). He also mentions Timothy, who we first met in the opening verses of Acts 16. You will remember that Timothy was the son of a Greek father and Jewish mother. He was a close friend throughout Paul's ministry and is mentioned twenty-four times in the New Testament.

It is possible that Timothy, who would be traveling back to Philippi with Epaphroditus, was also the secretary who took Paul's dictation and then carefully transcribed it in small, compact Greek script onto the rather expensive writing surfaces used for first-century letters.

Apparently, Paul's handwriting, as he tells his Galatian readers (Gal. 6:11), was too large, possibly the result of bad eyesight. But it was his practice to write a final greeting in his own hand at the end of his letters: "The salutation of Paul with mine own hand, which is the token in every epistle: so I write" (2 Thess. 3:17).

Paul begins now by describing himself and Timothy as

Letter to a Young Church.

15

"servants of Jesus Christ." It is clear from this that they saw themselves as servants or slaves of Jesus, who is the Christ—the Messiah. In other words, he immediately acknowledges in writing that Jesus is the messianic fulfillment of the promise in the Hebrew Scriptures.

He next adds to whom the letter is specifically written: "...All the saints in Christ Jesus which are at Philippi, with the bishops and deacons" (1:1). Paul uses the word *saints* here in the same general sense that he has used it elsewhere—saints were, and are, ordinary Christians. I've always been pleased with Paul's order here: He first mentions the ordinary Christians, the followers, and then he adds that the letter is for their leaders, too—the bishops and deacons.

In studying this marvelous letter, it is important that we remember it was written to real people in a real place. We can so easily forget in our study that Bible people were real. They weren't legendary, mythological characters who behaved according to the fancy of the storyteller. These were actual people with real problems—they were the church in Philippi.

As was mentioned in the Preface, the beginnings of this church were seen as Lydia, a businesswoman, a healed slave priestess of a Greek cult, and a prison guard and his family came together in fellowship (Acts 16). Then as others were added to that fellowship, it became necessary to establish a structure that included special leaders—overseers—and ministers. We see in this that Christians then, even as now, cannot live in isolation. We need fellowship with each other and that fellowship requires an order and structure. And as Paul stressed so heavily in his letters, fellowship, to be redemptive, must have unity.

I think, too, there is a great deal of significance in Paul's phrase "in Christ Jesus" in verse 1. The order and institutional nature of the Church is to be subject to the eternal Lordship of Jesus Christ. In other words, the Church isn't just *any* organization with prescribed leaders and followers. Rather, it is the mystery of our obedience to Jesus Christ and our living, day-by-day relationship with Him that enables us to be a part of the Church and the Church to fulfill its mission in the world.

I feel so often that we are in danger of holding too casual an attitude about the Church. We tend to be critical of it

A view of the port city of Kavalla—known as Neapolis in the first century—showing the Roman wall and aqueduct. It was here that Paul landed on his first visit to Macedonia (Acts 16:11). Neapolis fronted on the Aegean Sea and was the port city that served Philippi.

at times, but we need to be reminded that it is made up of imperfect people like ourselves. But ever since those first-century days, following the event of Pentecost, the Church has been and remains God's means of getting the message of Good News to hurting people.

Paul completes his opening greeting in verse 2, "Grace be unto you, and peace...." These are important words to Paul. "Grace" comes to us from a Greek word that means "surprise gift." It is an important part of Paul's love-vocabulary, and its original derivation comes from a word that means "joy."

The word peace is a beautiful word in Greek, but it is even more powerful in Hebrew. *Shalom* means more than the absence of war. Rather, it means health, wholeness, integration, and I believe this was at the heart of Paul's use of it here. His purpose in this part of the greeting was to unite the Jewish and Greek (non-Jew) aspirations into his wish for his friends—that they might know the surprise gift of love and the healthy peace that comes from God the Father and the Lord Jesus Christ. And, for Paul, it is his Lord who is the author of each gift.

Christian Partnership.

Paul next prays for those to whom he is writing (1:3–11). His pattern of prayer for his friends at Philippi might well be a model for us.

First Paul thanks God for "every remembrance of you" (1:3). This is an intensely personal letter, and as Paul is confined in the Roman prison and thinks about his friends in Philippi, he is filled with joy (1:4). Next he tells them that he is thankful for their fellowship—partnership—in the gospel (1:5). They have been, and are, his friends in the Lord, and for this he is thankful to God. The term Paul uses here to describe this relationship is familiar—*koinonia*, a Christian closeness that holds us together in Christ as partners.

Then he goes on to assure his friends of his confidence that the very God that began the good work in their lives will Himself complete it (1:6). Paul's point for his readers and us is that God has done something very concrete and real in our lives and that this will come to its completion at that future time when all of history converges into its final fulfillment in Christ.

That is what is meant by the phrase in verse 6, "the day of Jesus Christ." This important term is used by Paul some twenty times in his writings and it also appears fifteen times in the Gospels. It looks ahead with eager anticipation to the day of our Lord's final victory. This is the focal point for Paul. There is, of course, no suggestion in his words or actions that we in any way ease up on the important task of being and living and witnessing in the world in which we live now. But, along with Paul, our focal point is the future.

Paul then continues to share his deepest feelings of love for his readers in verses 7 and 8: "I have you in my heart.... I long after you...." He isn't ashamed to openly express his love and appreciation for their goodness and loyalty to him, and his feeling of longing for them carries an implication of "homesickness." For anyone who may have mistakenly thought Paul to be cold or distant or legalistic, this intimate look into his heart is most revealing.

Again, the tender Apostle is our model. We are frequently hesitant to be vulnerable. We wear masks intended to conceal who and what we are. We're afraid to express feelings of love and caring, even though we, like those around us, are starved to hear the words, "I love you." Paul was every inch a man, but there was none of the phony "macho" image about him.

Then, having expressed his own love for them he prays, "that your love may abound yet more and more in knowledge and in all judgment" (1:9). It is significant that he attached this love growth to "knowledge" and "judgment" —better translated "discernment" or "practical insight." In other words, he prays that their love will grow in ways of wise knowledge and practical insight.

I have been greatly impressed by Pastor Kyung Chik Han of the Young Nak Presbyterian Church in Seoul, Korea. Explaining in a meeting the examination process for elders in that church, he said that each prospective elder is examined in "Bible, theology, church history, and common sense." Those Korean Christians seem to have borrowed their four criteria for service from Paul's prayer for his Christian friends in Philippi. Their foundation in the knowledge of Christ is to be firm and strong, and they are to be sensible and thoughtful. Indeed, common sense is essential to Christian growth.

1. Paul is thankful for the fellowship of his close friends in Philippi.

2. He is thankful for their faithfulness as friends. They didn't forget him as time passed.

3. He has complete confidence that God will continue the "good work" that has been started in them. Paul knows God is faithful, and he affirms his belief in their faithfulness.

4. He prays that their love (*agape*) may continue to grow in knowledge and common sense in a way that honors God.

A Summary of Paul's Prayer.

RIGHT AND ABOVE. The Egnatian Road (Via Egnatia) near Philippi. Paul traveled over this road from Neapolis to Philippi. This old Roman road connected Rome with the eastern provinces of the Empire. A close look at the picture on the right shows the ruts from the ancient wagons and chariots.

5. In verses 10 and 11 Paul closes his prayer that they may be filled with the practical fruits of righteousness "which are by Jesus Christ, unto the glory and praise of God."

This prayer is vast in its possibilities, and yet, at its core, there is a wonderful simplicity—Paul's confidence affirming God's ability to complete what He starts.

The prayer asks for many things for his friends, and at the same time it asks for one thing—that their lives may be

filled in a very practical way with the Spirit of Christ. Stop a moment and re-read Galatians 5:22–23.

As we reflect on Paul's prayer for his intimate friends in Philippi, we see that it is equally fresh and up-to-date for us 1,900 years later. There is a marvelous constancy in Paul's writing!

Paul next gives his readers the assurance that "the things which happened unto me" have resulted for good (1:12–14). The words "in all the palace" in verse 13 are translated "Praetorian Guard" in other versions. This may give us a clue to the place of Paul's imprisonment at that time as well as to the extent of the outreach of his message.

The Gospel Penetrates High Places.

A number of Roman inscriptions have been located referring to the Praetorian Guard of the Caesars. This was a handpicked group of soldiers organized by Emperor Augustus in 2 B.C. to guard the palace. Whether this reference would indicate that Paul was imprisoned in the precincts of Nero's Palatium, the imperial house with its incredible maze of buildings, we cannot, however, know for certain.

Being in Prison—a Benefit.

Paul wants those of his readers who were worried about his safety to see here through his words that his imprisonment has not struck a destructive blow to the spread of the gospel. In fact, his being in prison has had two beneficial results.

First, Paul has evidently become a rather famous prisoner among the soldiers who guard him, and since so many of the people in Philippi were former Roman soldiers, he knows they would appreciate that development. He also indicates that his guards know that he is in prison because of his Christian teaching and preaching. They were far more impressed with that than they would have been if he had been held only on a legal technicality that originated in the distant city of Caesarea Philippi. And, of course, their interest gave Paul a greater opportunity for witnessing.

Then he goes on to say that "many of the brethren in the Lord, waxing confident by my bonds, are much more bold to speak the word without fear" (1:14). In other words, despite Paul's imprisonment, the other believers were bolder in their witness because of the way Paul handled his own circumstances.

The irony of what was happening in Rome was remarkable. A political tyrant with the use of force and terror had imprisoned Paul and was trying to stamp out the Christian movement, but, in reality, his actions had so stirred up the believers that they were even bolder and without fear. There is a modern-day equivalent of that in Poland. There the Solidarity movement was bolder and spoke out with greater impact when its senior leader, Lech Walesa, was in prison than when he was free from harassment.

Probably most of us have experienced the rather scary fact that our Christian growth is often enhanced by going through difficult and hard times. I have a writer friend who somewhat reluctantly admits that his best writing usually comes out of periods when he is hurting the most.

In verse 15 Paul tells his readers that while most of the Christians in Rome were being faithful to their commitment, there were those who preached "Christ even of envy and strife" (1:15). He doesn't identify these people except to describe their motives. There can be no question that they caused Paul concern, but then he comes up with a somewhat surprising twist. He takes the position in verse 18 that even though their motives may not be right or pure, the very fact that the gospel is preached is good.

Doing Right for the Wrong Reasons.

From this we see that Paul is convinced that Jesus Christ is able to break through the most hostile settings in order to make Himself known. Most certainly, in his own ministry, especially at Corinth, Paul had learned that sometimes even the most negative circumstances can result in the most dramatic open doors for the gospel.

A particularly outstanding example of this occurred on his trip to Rome when his prison ship was wrecked at Malta. Through that mishap Paul had a significant ministry with the ship's crew as well as with residents of the island (Acts 27–28).

When Disaster Was Turned into Success.

Of course it is serious when the message of the gospel is distorted. But in an ironic way even the distorters may actually play a special role in preparing people for the truth. Their chaotic and self-serving picture of Christianity often presents just that contrast to the straightforwardness of an authentic message in a way that heightens the appeal of the true gospel.

For example, in 1968 our family toured Russia. While in Leningrad we visited the Museum of Religion and Atheism. The displays offered a heavy-handed portrayal of the Soviet-Communist interpretation of the history of the Russian Orthodox Church. Every effort was made to picture Russian Christians as foolish, superstitious, and morally bankrupt hypocrites.

After viewing those displays, however, I had a very good feeling about the future of Christianity in Russia. I thought to myself, "With enemies like these, who needs friends!" I could just imagine the confusion of the Russian secularist when he or she meets Christians and discovers they are not foolish, superstitious, and hypocritical. Such a confrontation with the Russian deception and attack on Christianity could result in helping the cause of Christ in the long run.

That is precisely the story of Ivan's experience in Aleksandr Solzhenitsyn's *One Day in the Life of Ivan Denisovich.* In the story, the cynic Ivan meets the young Christian Alyosha, who doesn't fit the negative expectations that Ivan has of Christians. This is but another case where good comes when evil is intended. It is this kind of wisdom and maturity that kept Paul from being overly concerned when the purity of the gospel presentation was marred. He knew—and we can learn this lesson from him—that God is in charge and that we can leave the consequences up to Him. We are to be ever alert but avoid playing God.

Paul's Need of Prayer.

At the same time Paul wants his friends in Philippi to know that he is in constant need of their prayers. He well understands both the power and the mystery of prayer: As they intercede for him in far-off Philippi, the Holy Spirit will minister to him in his Roman prison cell. In effect, Paul is saying here that by their prayers and the help of the Holy Spirit he expects "deliverance" in spite of his circumstances.

Other versions substitute the word "help" in the place of "supply" in verse 19. It is rather interesting that the word for help comes from a Greek root that means chorus. Following through on this idea, we hear Paul saying that the Holy Spirit "choruses" the parts together and makes them adequate. This idea of the chorusing ministry of the Holy Spirit has greatly enriched my need for and appreciation of group intercessory prayer.

Paul knows full well that it is through prayer that he will not "be ashamed," that he will have the courage to stand firm in the midst of the dangers and stresses that threaten him (1:20). We, like Paul, face the subtleties of living in a society that often seems to call for compromise if we are to make it. For any of us to neglect prayer is dangerous, and we all need the prayer support of Christian friends.

A Ringing Affirmation.

We come now to some of Paul's loftiest words as he writes, "For to me to live is Christ, and to die is gain" (1:21). With these words, Paul seems now (1:21–26) to open himself up to his readers in a remarkable way. There is no sense of resignation or fatalism in these verses. Instead

The acropolis in the Macedonian city of Philippi. The city was named after Philip II of Macedon. After Philippi was conquered by the Romans in 168 B.C., Philippi was made a Roman colony where discharged army veterans settled. Citizens of Philippi were Roman citizens with full rights.

they are the realistic result of his journey with Christ as Savior and Lord and Friend.

He has trusted his present life or death into the hands of God, and in faith he trusts everything out ahead to the One who has kept him this far. At the same time he believes that he still has an unfinished task, so there's no hint of a death wish here. He is well aware of his God-given abilities, and he intends to completely abandon himself to his calling in Christ—living every moment to the fullest and without any fear of death. We see in Paul the healthy balance of a person who is realistic about the present and the future and who possesses a realism founded on complete confidence in God. I think John Calvin's understanding of this verse is significant. He took exception with those who believed that Paul was saying that death itself would be gain for him. Instead Calvin felt that it was Christ that would be gain to Paul *either in life or death*. The focus was intended to be on Christ.

There is a wonderfully fresh matter-of-factness about Paul in these sentences that makes this part of Philippians very helpful and healing to us. We find reassurance here also that as we come to the end of our lives—whenever that happens—we do not face an empty, inky abyss. Instead, we find there the same Lord Jesus that we have known in all of the earlier circumstances of our lives.

Finally, in verses 25 and 26, Paul seems to be telling the Philippians that it is his hope that he will continue to be with them and he also hopes to visit them again as a means of being helpful. And it is also his hope that in all things they will see Christ in him. Again, in these words, Paul models what is meant to be the highest purpose in our lives: to live here and now so that those around us—our family and friends—may see Christ in our words and actions.

A Call to Discipleship.

As we move now toward the close of this particular lesson, we seem to hear Paul calling the Christians at Philippi to discipleship. Our King James text says, "Only let your conversation be as it becometh the gospel of Christ" (1:27). Other versions update the language to say that we are to live in such a way as to be worthy of the gospel. These words remind us of Ephesians 4:1: "...that ye walk worthy of the vocation wherewith ye are called." As Christians, we are called *to live out* the Good News that we have experienced.

I believe we have in these words an evangelical ethic that is distinctive in the New Testament. We aren't told to *be good* or warned to *do good* in response to guilt or fear. Instead, we are first told that we are loved and then that we are to live out that love toward others in a real and practical sense.

It is rather interesting that the word translated "conversation" or "manner of life" in verse 27 has political overtones in the Greek. Instead of "conversation" or "manner of life," it could accurately read "your citizen life" or "your political life."

The idea being expressed to the Christians at Philippi is that as individuals who have inescapable individual responsibilities, we also have a common social responsibility to live the Christian life in its truest sense within the community and society. In other words, Paul does not draw a distinction between a *personal gospel* of salvation through Christ and a *public gospel*.

Then, in addition to all the instructions he has given so far, Paul now says that we aren't to be "terrified" by the forces of evil that confront us as we try to live for the Lord. We're not to panic, but to hold steady in confidence. This observation ties right in with a fact of history—when a source of tyranny has lost its ability to produce panic or immobilizing fear, it has lost its power over us.

The closing words in this first chapter tell us that as Christians we are involved in a grand contest against evil and fear—the powers of death and the power of the devil. This contest goes with our discipleship, with our forgiveness, and with our experience of God's love. When we place our complete trust in God's character, we enter the contest. By our own choosing, we are on His team and we are in the game. We are committed, but the Good News is that we are on the right team.

In this lesson Paul has opened himself up to us in a moving and amazing way—he has shared with us his philosophy of life. And it is a contagious philosophy because at its center is the radical possibility of a human being in relationship with the living Lord. When that philosophy is understood as Paul understood it, it is an awesome possibility!

Heavenly Father, Help me to live "worthy of the gospel"—in a manner consistent with the teachings of Your Word. Help me to live out the gospel in experience within my community and society at large. Amen.

WHAT THIS SCRIPTURE MEANS TO ME—Philippians 1

Letters can be so important in our lives. I remember writing letters to my grandmother Cook when I was in the first grade. I'd lie on my tummy on the scratchy living room rug with a tablet and pencil. Then I'd tell my mother what I wanted to say, and she would spell each word aloud for me as I laboriously printed in large capital letters. And at the end I always included lots of O O O O's and X X X X's—hugs and kisses.

When Grandmother Cook died at age ninety-four, we discovered that she had saved every letter I had written her.

Isn't it marvelous that the church at Philippi saved Paul's letter and that it has been preserved through hundreds of years for us to read today? Like my grandmother and the Philippian Christians, I too have saved letters that Christian friends have written to me.

When I was a teenager I attended a Christian conference in Georgia every summer. One of the popular youth leaders was Mr. E. E. Lee of Dallas, Texas. His nickname was "Hot Dog" because he used that expression so often! We always enjoyed his classes because he kept us laughing. But we also learned a lot from him. The thing I remember most about Mr. Lee was he always wrote to me between summers. His letters were a great encouragement as I grew in my Christian faith.

As I've thought about how my own life has been enriched by letters from Christian friends, I've been impressed by just how important it is to be faithful in my own letter writing. We never know when a note of appreciation and affirmation may be just the encouragement a friend needs. Paul seemed to understand that, and while his letters always contained some instruction, they were also full of encouragement.

One special word of encouragement that Paul wrote to his friends in Philippi is the promise in 1:6, "He which hath begun a good work in you will perform it until the day of Jesus Christ." That verse reminds me of a plaque our son's Sunday school teacher gave him when he was quite young. It read: "Please be patient. God hasn't finished with me yet." Those were wise words, not only for our son, but for his mother as well.

Then, too, I'm sure Paul's readers were greatly encouraged to learn in this letter that he was all right—even though he was a prisoner in Rome. In fact, he told them some good things were happening because he was a prisoner. The elite guards who were with him night and day were hearing the Good News about Jesus Christ. In addition, many of his Christian friends were working extra hard to witness and teach because Paul wasn't free to get around. It's interesting, isn't it, how God can so often bring good from experiences that in themselves are not good.

Our friend Howard Hayes is a prime example of good coming out of a not-so-good situation. He cared lovingly and faithfully for his cancer-ridden wife until her death. Then, even though he had cancer himself, he set out to be of help to out-of-town cancer patients who came to our city for treatment at the medical center. Outpatients and their families often were there for weeks and months for treatment.

Because Howard saw the need, he encouraged our church to provide ten furnished apartments to rent at cost. And he volunteered to manage the details of the rentals. In the several years before his death he was instrumental in helping hundreds of people.

Certainly no one would ever say that it was good in itself that Howard and his wife had cancer. But out of that experience God used Howard to help many people who were in desperate need.

I find great encouragement in knowing that if I let Him, God can turn some of my difficult times into blessings. No experience—even a bad one—is wasted in God's economy.

LESSON 2
PHILIPPIANS 2

The Hymn of Gratitude
to the Servant Lord

Dear God, My thanks are inadequate; my gratitude insufficient. And yet I thank You for sending Jesus to be my Savior. Thank You for Your blessed assurance. AMEN.

A Problem in the Church. The opening verses for our Scripture in this lesson tell us that a problem had developed in the church at Philippi (2:1–4). Tensions had arisen within the congregation, and people were taking sides for and against each other. Toward the end of the letter Paul actually names three people within the congregation who may be the ones involved in the differences that now endangered the unity of the church.

Controversies and disunity in churches are certainly not new. They occurred in the New Testament churches as each of Paul's letters tells us. This may come as a surprise to us because of our tendency to idealize the beginnings of Christianity. But our study of Paul's letters so far clearly indicates the early presence of church squabbles. These squabbles provide both negative and positive lessons for us.

First, of course, it is terribly unfortunate that very early in the life of the Christian fellowship there was any conflict that could threaten the believers' life in Christ and the effective witness of the Church in the world. Such "in house" struggles are a wasteful use of energy and time that should be spent creatively in winning new Christians and nurturing young believers.

But even while this was going on in the Philippian church, we see that it is this very fragile fellowship that God was using to make help available to the hungry and destitute Christians in Jerusalem. And it was this same shaky group that was constantly giving support to Paul, their mentor in the Lord. And so we can take courage, in spite of the flaws of disunity and strong-willed interpersonal controversies that always seem to be a part of our church life, that God can use us even as He did the church at Philippi to bring about His purposes in the world.

In a way, I suspect we can credit early church conditions for these letters of Paul. Had there not been problems, we might not have the richness and insight of the great Apostle's experience in the Lord. It is impossible for me to imagine our not having this intensely personal and warm letter that we're studying now. But one of the reasons we have it is because of the problems that developed in Philippi.

Another plus for us in having Paul's writings as a part of our New Testament is that from them we see that the early church was far from perfect, but it was made up of flesh and blood people just like ourselves. They, like us, were struggling to understand what it meant to be a Christian in a pagan world. And they, like us, in their quest for spiritual maturity frequently fell short of being what God wanted them to be. Yet, it was Christians just like those at Philippi that the Lord used to spread the gospel across the world and to establish churches—places of fellowship— where the witness of the Good News could be given. We in turn can be encouraged because the same Lord that was with the Philippian church in the first century is with us today. That same power—His power—is ours.

It is also helpful for us to realize that the problems that were present at Philippi and Colossae have their parallels in each generation. And the same positive discoveries of faith, hope, and love that were a response to their problems apply to our generation as well.

It is this shared community of our common humanity and the same living presence of Christ that make all the letters of the New Testament contemporary documents for the Christian Church in every age and time. For example, in the case of the church in Philippi we know from a letter written to them by Polycarp in A.D. 110 that the

Philippian Christians were still struggling with problems of disunity—Ignatius, another early church father, termed it "factionalism."

Encouragement Therapy.

We come next to a close look at just how Paul decided to deal with the factions and disunity at Philippi. This is important to us because the same principles that Paul used there are still very up-to-date and will work now for us.

Our Scripture lesson opens as Paul writes, "If there be therefore any consolation in Christ, if any comfort of love, if any fellowship of the Spirit, if any bowels and mercies" (2:1). The word "consolation" that appears in this verse in our King James text is translated "encouragement" in many of the later versions.

The Greek word Paul used here actually means "to call alongside" or "come alongside." A form of this word is used in the Gospel of John for the Holy Spirit, the promised Comforter who comes "alongside" and teaches us about Christ.

The words of encouragement that Paul brings together in verses 1 and 2 are connected by the repetitious impact of the word "if." In thinking about the difficulties that plague their fellowship, Paul wants his readers to concentrate their thinking on this series of "if's":

1. IF they have experienced in Christ a specific "coming alongside" companionship—any encouragement.

2. IF they have experienced any motivational strengthening from love.

3. IF they have experienced fellowship *(koinonia)* in the Holy Spirit.

4. IF they have experienced that warm affection and love from deep within themselves that expresses itself in tenderness and love in their actions toward others.

In other words, Paul is asking them to remember and picture the positive experiences of God's love at work in their lives. This is a deliberate effort on his part in establishing a mood or frame of mind that he will ask them to contrast with the controversy and negativism that is making them critical of each other and ruining their feelings of oneness in Christ. Here we see the Apostle Paul as the real originator of the power of positive thinking—a term brought up-to-date and made popular by Dr. Norman Vincent Peale.

The Agora or central marketplace at Philippi as seen from the acropolis.

Paul's method here is sound as he asks his readers to decide for themselves whether they will build their lives on the specific experiences of encouragement they have enjoyed in Christ and with each other, or, whether they will ignore those enriching experiences and continue to be involved in the destructive divisions in the church.

Paul, of course, expresses the hope that they will choose the way of love in their relationship with their fellow Christians (2:2). But he is realistic about what that will cost them—they will lose the right to feel and express any kind of superiority over anyone else in their fellowship. Paul makes it clear that in his opinion a pattern of encouragement is best, but it demands humility and genuine concern for their brothers and sisters in the Lord.

Admittedly, the attitude and way of encouragement that Paul is writing about here is difficult and costly. In fact, from a natural point of view, it is impossible. It is utterly impossible except for Jesus Christ, who Himself is our model for both humility and encouragement. This is why Paul writes, "Let this mind be in you, which was also in Christ Jesus" (2:5).

As I try to understand as best I can this particular chapter and lesson—the greatest chapter on Christ in all of Paul's writings—I have come to believe that at first Paul had planned just a simple statement on how Christ through His life of humility has encouraged us. But then, I suspect, as he reflected further he decided a few simple words were not enough, and he launched into the New Testament's greatest hymn to the person and ministry of Jesus Christ. What had begun as a brief mention or an uncomplicated illustration became a majestic song of wonder at the love of God. This is one of those times when Paul's genius with words is almost unmatched.

Jesus—the Servant Lord.

In verse 6 Paul opens this grand hymn to the Lord with these words: "Who, [Jesus] being in the form of God, thought it not robbery to be equal with God." Paul is telling us here that Jesus had God's very nature—He possessed God's attributes; He possessed God's character. Other translations of this verse give us the idea that equality with God did not have to be seized or grasped because Jesus already had it. I suggest you stop for a few moments and read this verse in several modern translations. In fact, I believe you will find it helpful before going on to read this entire hymn of praise to Jesus (2:5–11) in several different translations. Each one will likely open up fresh truth.

The crescendo of praise reaches new heights in verse 7 as Paul writes that Jesus "made himself of no reputation, and took upon him the form of a servant, and was made in the likeness of men." Again, later versions cast light on this as they refer to Jesus "emptying" Himself ("made himself of no reputation"). This doesn't mean that He emptied Himself of His divine nature. Rather, I believe the reference is to rank or privilege, to the glories that were His. And with that emptying Jesus took on the essential form of a servant/slave and was born "in the likeness of men."

Paul has given us a colorful picture here of the One who has the essence of a slave and is really like us as a human being, but at the same time He is the One who from the beginning has been of the original being of God. Here we see the uncompromised total humanity and total deity of Jesus Christ.

And in verse 8 we read that this same Jesus who has "humbled himself" was also "obedient unto death" on the cross. Through His "emptying" and becoming like a man, Jesus had identified fully with us in life. And now we read that His final identification was that of His own death. This we too understand because we all die.

But Jesus' death was different. For the first-century Roman or Jew, death on a cross was punishment for wrongs that deserved death. The only thing Jesus was guilty of, however, was identification with the human family. It is the tragedy, the sin, the lostness of human beings that Jesus took on Himself, and that divine humiliation has now broken the steel-like grasp of sin and death on human life.

Paul next moves on (2:9) to give us the greatest surprise of all—humiliation was not defeat! It was a victory—final victory over sin and death. This is another one of those glorious paradoxes of our faith: the humble are exalted, the first shall be last, to lose life is to find it, Jesus the Servant becomes the conquering Lord.

Next, we are told that Jesus was not only exalted but also "given a name which is above every name." In the first century a person's name signified his or her dignity and distinct character. Indeed, Jesus has the character and dignity above all others, not only on earth, the creation we understand, but also in heaven, the creation beyond our understanding. And there is no name in the shadowy realms of the demonic or the places of death that has more power or mystery than that of Jesus (2:10).

In this magnificent hymn to Jesus we see Him exalted as the Last Word, as the Lord over life and death and over heaven and hell. And now we come to verse 11—one of the grandest and most significant verses in our New Testament: "And that every tongue should confess that Jesus Christ is Lord, to the glory of God the Father." The literal meaning of the word "confess" in this verse is "agree." So what Paul is saying is that the time is coming when everyone will *agree* that Jesus Christ is Lord, "to the glory of God." In other words, it was Jesus' purpose to direct the full attention of the human race to God. And His purpose becomes ours; to Him be the glory for everything!

There is every indication from the style, rhythm, and vocabulary of these verses (2:6–11) that this was an early hymn of the Church about Jesus Christ. We have no hint as to who composed the hymn—it may have been Paul, but then again it could well have been some other early Christian writer. It really doesn't matter, though. The important thing to us in our study is that the words, whoever wrote them, conformed perfectly to Paul's understanding of Jesus. In addition, it is extremely important that we agree that "Jesus Christ is Lord" over our lives.

"Work Out Your Own Salvation."

Paul moves now from the Christ-hymn to some very practical matters as he writes that we are to work out our salvation with fear and trembling (2:12). Because of God's prior act in our favor we are to make God's act our own. Paul's intent here, I believe, is that God's grace must work itself out through our lives. This is a grand freedom sentence that points up the intensely personal responsibility of working through the implications of Christ's salvation in all the corridors and living rooms and small passageways of our lives.

No one can work out our salvation for us; we must do it for ourselves. And since Paul is fully aware of the urgency of this, he adds two other words to this freedom text: "fear" and "trembling." The implication here is that we are to be fearfully alert and awake—deadly serious—as we

A view of the acropolis at Philippi showing the ruins of an ancient wall.

work out our salvation, as we grow and mature in the Christian faith.

It is important, however, that we understand Paul is not telling his friends in Philippi to earn their salvation by fearful and wakeful work. There is no hidden theology of "salvation by works" in this letter. Paul is always careful to make it clear that God's love and forgiveness come first—His grace precedes our response. But he also makes it clear that we are to respond to God's love with reverence and alertness.

Paul then adds, "For it is God which worketh in you both to will and to do of his good pleasure" (2:13). God is at work in us! This is the exciting Good News that makes it possible for us to work out our own salvation.

There is an intriguing double use of the word "work" in these exciting sentences. Paul has combined the freedom of our faith by which, on one side, we turn the free salvation we have in Christ into a concrete action by our work and efforts. Then, on the other side, Paul reminds us that God is also at work in us every step of the way. This means that while our salvation is a gift, which we could never earn, we work out its meaning in every part of our lives. Augustine, the early church father, put this idea into a prayer: "O God, Thou who art ever at rest and ever at work, may we be ever at rest and at work."

In all of this we discover that what at first seemed to be a contradiction is not one at all. In fact, the human experience of two people falling in love is very much like this marvelous "contradiction." There is a sense of rest in the experience of being a receiver of love and acceptance and commitment. But at the same time there is the good work that must inevitably follow as the two lovers make plans, inform friends, save money for future dreams, and make wedding arrangements with the church—all of this is worked out with fear and trembling.

But there is no idea of earning the other's love through all of this work and effort. The gift of love came first, and the work was the natural consequence that followed love. They go together.

But there's a significant distinction here. The way we respond to receiving salvation through Jesus Christ is extremely different from the way we handle some of the other "givens" in our lives. Let's face it, there wouldn't be much fear and trembling involved in a change of schedule of the No. 7 bus that we usually take at 4:15, but which now leaves at 4:22. Falling in love, however, is far more earth-shaking, as is hearing the news of the birth of a son or daughter. But learning that we are loved by the Lord who has a Name above every other name is the most radical discovery of all!

As Paul continues his instructions in verse 15, he tells his readers that they are to "be blameless and harmless [innocent], the sons of God, without rebuke [blemish], in the midst of a crooked and perverse nation, among whom ye shine as lights in the world."

"Ye Shine as Lights in the World."

When I first read those words, it seemed like a terribly unequal match. On one side we see a group of Christians who are not to grumble but be trusting. They were blameless and innocent like children. But the group on the opposing side are crooked (devious) and perverse (highly trained in evil ways). They give every appearance of being as unevenly matched as two teams playing with different sets of rules.

But then Paul moves ahead to tell his Philippian friends that they have two weapons that are more potent than the weapons of evil; they have "light" (2:15) and "life" (2:16). They have the power of faith and the power of life. Now the balance in the match is different.

For example, if I were to pick a winner in a karate match, I would choose the person who knows the truth—the skill—of the event as opposed to the person who plans to win with an illegal and devious hit. The reasoning behind this kind of thinking is that people who have to break the rules in order to win usually do so because they are less skillful. When an honest player is aware of the presence of deception, the match is tilted away from the crooked player to the one who understands the truth or skill of the event.

And so, with an athletic tone Paul has warned his readers that in facing a contest with the powers of evil they will come up against all sorts of illegal maneuvers. But they are not to fight fire with fire, nor are they to become involved with illegal countermoves, but they are to follow the rules of the game.

The Christian strategy never involves deception or un-

The ruins of an ancient church in Philippi. When Paul first arrived in Philippi, there wasn't even a Jewish synagogue. The people met to worship in the open air by the river.

derhanded methods. The ends do not justify deceptive means. A strategy of truthfulness and honesty may appear at times to be slower, but it is ultimately better because we never need to cover our tracks or remember different stories.

In addition to the weapon of light or truth, Paul mentions the weapon of life. The "word of life" means there is the possibility of forgiveness, of new life, of life in Christ. Against this, no opposing force can prevail!

As sometimes happens in Paul's writing, there now seems to be a rather sudden shift of mood (2:17–18): "Yea, and if I be offered upon the sacrifice...." He seems to be speaking of his own danger and of the possibility that he may not be released from Nero's Roman prison as he had hoped. Even though he refers to his possible death, there is no note of depression over his present situation, and he speaks again of the joy he gets from thinking about them.

With special reason, Paul devotes the final words in this chapter (2:19–30) to his two friends, who will be traveling together from Rome to Philippi. Timothy will be making a pastoral visit, while Epaphroditus will be traveling home. The sensitivity of Paul's words here gives us a remarkable study of the skillful handling of a potentially embarrassing situation.

My Friends—Timothy and Epaphroditus.

His comments about Timothy are straightforward and to the point (2:19–24). Paul is looking forward to Timothy's visit with them so he can then return to Rome with news of the congregation at Philippi along with a report on the other churches in Macedonia. It is easy, too, to see in Paul's words here that his confidence in Timothy is very great.

His comments about Epaphroditus seem to be carefully chosen because Paul is most anxious to convey his deep feelings. This young man had been sent earlier by the church at Philippi to be of help and service to Paul. But now the young missionary is returning, ill and evidently homesick. And apparently, Epaphroditus is concerned because of his inability to stay longer and complete his mission.

Sensitive to the young man's feelings, Paul is now writing to prepare the way for Epaphroditus to return home without losing face before his friends and family in the church. Paul assumes all responsibility for sending the young man home and then adds lavish but obviously sincere praise for his missionary efforts. What a marvelous example the Apostle is to us here. It is much more redemptive to build others up than to tear them down. At best, human relationships within the Church are fragile. We all need affirmation and praise—not criticism. And Paul gives us a beautiful model of Christian grace as he speaks of his young friend.

In fact, he urges the people at Philippi not only to welcome Epaphroditus but to honor him and "hold such in reputation" (2:29). This is the same idea as is conveyed by the fifth commandment, which instructs us to honor our parents. Now, Paul uses this very same word for the way he hoped the church would receive the young short-term missionary back into their fellowship. It is obvious that Paul loves this young man, and he is anxious for Epaphroditus to be received in love.

I think the real test of Christian love and character is in how a leader treats those with whom he or she is working. Most certainly, Paul scores high in this test. He is a splendid model of leadership as he shows affectionate concern for his young colleague in his anxiety to spare him any embarrassment. Once again we have gained valuable insight into the heart and feelings of Paul as we attempt to live each day in a way that will bring honor to the Lord as we act out our faith in the real world.

Lord, Help me to live today, all day, in Your presence, moment by moment, offering every deed as an act of devotion to You, bringing You honor and pleasure. Amen.

WHAT THIS SCRIPTURE MEANS TO ME—Philippians 2

JOY is the key word in Philippians. Even though Paul was in prison and even though he was intensely concerned over the lack of harmony among his fellow Christians in the churches he had founded, he was still full of joy.

As I read this Scripture lesson, I couldn't help asking, "How could Paul be so happy and full of joy at this time of his life?"

One reason for Paul's joy, I believe, was his vital relationship with Christ. Although he was in prison, restricted by Roman chains and far away from loved ones, Paul could still say, "Jesus Christ is Lord." He knew even under those circumstances that Christ would continue to work in his life and in the lives of those around him.

Then, too, I think Paul was happy and full of joy because he just naturally had an attitude of gratitude. Instead of concentrating on the freedom he had lost and all the other things he didn't have, Paul felt a genuine appreciation for the gifts the Christians at Philippi had sent and for the messenger who had brought them. From all of this, he knew his friends loved him and were praying for him.

Joy in life really seems to be bound up in relationships rather than in circumstances. I remember an acrostic my childhood Sunday school teacher wrote on the chalkboard. She put the letters *J O Y* one under the other. Then she said, "If you want to know the secret of real joy, watch what I write next."

By the *J* she wrote *Jesus.*

By the *O* she wrote *Others.*

By the *Y* she wrote *You.*

Then she said, "You'll only know true joy when you give priority to Jesus first, others second, and yourself last."

It has been many years since I first saw that acrostic, but the happiest times in my life have been when I remembered that I need to keep Jesus, others, and myself in the right relationship. Many of the problems Paul was concerned about in the Philippian church would have been solved if their relationship priorities had been in that order.

I recall so well when a friend of my father read a book entitled *Looking Out for Number One.* He told my father it had changed his life—and it certainly had. He left his wife of many years and started living with someone else's wife. He claimed that the time had come for him to take charge of his life and get some happiness.

But it didn't work out the way he thought it would. In the wake of his foolish and sinful decision he left a heartbroken wife, a wronged husband, and a shocked and grieving church. And his children carried wounds that never seemed to heal. Making self the center of life doesn't produce pure joy.

When my husband was a young minister, he was asked to preach during a week of meetings at a little church in the mountains of New Mexico. This congregation had recently split off from another one. But after listening to the gospel for a week, they voted to disband and reunite with their former church. Those folks in that little church put into practice Paul's advice to his friends in Philippi, "Fulfil ye my joy, that ye be likeminded, having the same love, being of one accord, of one mind. Let nothing be done through strife or vainglory; but in lowliness of mind let each esteem other better than themselves" (2:2–3).

Something else that gave Paul a great deal of joy during those prison days came in watching the spiritual growth of Timothy, his trusted "son in the ministry." I remember the first time I experienced a similar feeling. Gloria was a nine-year-old girl in the first church training group I ever conducted. I enjoyed watching her grow up and mature as a Christian. We kept in touch throughout all of her school years. And I was as thrilled as she was when she learned sign language so she could interpret the church services for the deaf.

Later Gloria married a minister and became an effective helper for him. Because of my mentor relationship with her, her achievements and happiness were a great source of joy for me.

LESSON 3
PHILIPPIANS 3

The Grand Design—
Paul as Our Model

Abba Father, You are the source of my joy! Sometimes I think my rejoicing depends on other things: success, money, good health, or being current with the latest fads. Thank You for reminding me that I can always rejoice in You. Amen.

Paul opens this third chapter as if he had every intention of moving rather quickly toward the end of the letter. And as we often try to do with our own letters, it looks as if he plans to end it on a high note—one of joy: "Finally, my brethren, rejoice in the Lord" (3:1).

Although he is undergoing the rigors of prison life, Paul's attitude is one of joy. Then, too, he knows his readers are undergoing stress and may even be forced to suffer persecution for their faith in the days ahead. But whatever the outer circumstances, Paul urges his readers to be full of joy in the Lord.

Paul is a colorful writer, but throughout all of his letters we find a rather spontaneous and even impulsive quality to his writing. At times, he even seems to interrupt himself and his thought progression as something different and important comes to mind. That is evidently happening here (3:2–3) as he takes on a very severe tone.

Finally…Rejoice.

A Change of Tone and a Warning.

First, he tells his readers to "beware of dogs" (3:2). This reference to dogs is always very abusive and negative when it appears in both the Old and New Testaments. In the Old Testament it implies chaotic uncleanness (see Deut. 23:18).

In anger over King Saul's pursuit of him, for example, David lashes out and says in effect, "Who are you chasing? a dead dog or a flea?" (see 1 Sam. 24:14). And twice in Psalm 22 the reference to dogs has to do with the most villainous attack on a person. It is clear from any and all of these references that the dog, in biblical times, was considered about the lowest form of life.

We know, also, from a number of rather graphic New Testament references and other first-century sources that the word "dog" was used by Jews as a degrading description of non-Jews—"gentile dogs." In fact, the rabbis of that day were fond of saying, "The nations of the world are like dogs."

And so it is more than a little ironic that Paul would take this term and direct it toward Jews who were making trouble and causing division by their insistence that non-Jewish Christians should follow the old Jewish practices, including the rite of circumcision. Paul's colorful choice of language here is quite surprising. I don't believe he necessarily intended to shock his readers, but he wanted desperately to get their attention as he now moved ahead to handle a serious theological matter.

We already know from our studies in Galatians and from the record of the first church council in Jerusalem (Acts 15) that an early controversy within the first-century church was the question of non-Jewish converts becoming subject to the Jewish Law. The question that rocked the young churches was simply this: Was it necessary for a non-Jewish believer in Christ to become Jewish as a vital part of his or her journey of faith? Paul, of course, was the leader in trying to resolve this controversy.

He had made it abundantly clear that he valued his Jewish heritage. And, as you will recall from our Acts studies, Paul approved of Timothy's being circumcised because even though his father was Greek, his mother was a Jew (Acts 16:1–3). But when Paul saw the extremist views of the Christian Jews in Jerusalem and how they had distorted the gospel of grace by insisting that non-Jewish converts

A very old church in the ruins of Philippi, identified in 1956 as a basilica. The place of worship for Christians in Paul's time was in the home of one of the believers.

be circumcised and follow the other provisions of the Law, he took a firm stand against them. He, in fact, refused to allow Titus, a Christian gentile, to be circumcised (Gal. 2:1–5). And Paul defended his position by insisting that to act otherwise would have reflected on the integrity of the gospel of grace.

While this question had been settled at the Jerusalem council by their decisions, "...but we believe that through the grace of the Lord Jesus Christ we shall be saved, even as they....Wherefore my sentence is, that we trouble not them, which from among the Gentiles are turned to God"

(Acts 15:11, 19)—there was slowness to accept that decision. Bad theory and bad practice seem to linger on even when the Church has decided on a greater truth. This is precisely why the Church in every generation needs the purifying and correcting ministry of sound teaching and doctrine. We are always in danger of going astray by taking teaching out of context or chasing after half-truths. It is dreadfully easy to baptize our prejudices and call them convictions.

False Teachers Invade Philippi.

It is very clear from Paul's words here that false teachers had arrived in Philippi and were urging the male Christians to show their devotion to Christ by being circumcised. And here, as in Corinth and the Asian churches, these false teachers accused Paul of being soft and a compromiser, and their accusations were evidently well flavored with proof texts from the Jewish Scriptures. Paul understood the subtleties of this approach and vigorously attacked the false teaching.

Unfortunately, such false teachers, with their distortions of the faith, did not disappear from the church scene in the first century. We are still plagued with people who take a partial truth and build a whole cult around it. So-called new movements that teach "new" truth appear frequently and even invade orthodox groups, and at times the "ring of truth" deceives well-meaning people for a while.

This is precisely why we must be soundly grounded in our faith through the study of God's Word, prayer, and close fellowship with caring Christians. Without that support we can so easily fall for some form of "distorted" truth.

We, like the Christians at Philippi, can be greatly helped at this point by Paul's pastoral advice. He puts the whole matter into perspective in one clearly worded sentence: "For we are the [true or authentic] circumcision, which worship God in the spirit, and rejoice in Christ Jesus, and have no confidence in the flesh" (3:3). In other words, the point Paul is making here is that it is only the Christians who are really circumcised, for theirs is of the heart.

Not Legalism, but Christ.

In these sentences, Paul reminds his Philippian friends that the true and complete fulfillment of the Law and the prophets and all the symbolic rituals that accompanied Old Testament tradition is found in Jesus Christ. He is the fulfillment of Abraham's covenant. And since this is true, we receive in Christ all the richness of God's promises.

Our task now is to *listen* to the Law and the prophets through Christ. In this way, we learn about observance of all the commandments by listening to what Jesus said about them. It is through our trust in Christ that we become wise enough not to place confidence in the special acts or procedures of any new legalism—whether that legalism is of our making or comes from someone else. And our ability to resist and overcome all forms of false teaching, no matter how pure they sound, comes through growth in the Christ of Resurrection Power!

The great and practical message to us from this part of our lesson is that we are to "worship God in the spirit, and rejoice in Christ Jesus" (3:3). This is our responsibility—no more, and no less. Paul's warning here is to "beware," "watch out" for anything else.

Paul's Credentials.

After the vigorous attack that Paul had made against the false teachers, and his insistence that it is really the Christians who are the true sons of Abraham because of their inner circumcision, he gives us a few sentences to establish his authority to write as he has (3:4–6). Yes, he is a Christian, but he is also a Jew. The personal style in this brief autobiographical account is quite characteristic in each of his letters.

In this respect, it seems to me that as a New Testament writer Paul is most like Jeremiah, the Old Testament prophet, in contrast to, for example, John, whom I would compare with the prophet Isaiah. Both John and Isaiah are much more private in their writing and keep their own personal life and feelings to themselves. But Paul and Jeremiah tell all. As we read these two writers, we learn a great deal about them and their feelings. Their personal, open, and first-person style is very much in vogue today. We like to know what a writer thinks and feels. But, above all, we like to know the background of a writer and his or her authority to write on a particular subject.

What Paul writes now is emotionally charged and even a bit humorous. First, he tells us that from a first-century Pharisaic assessment of mighty acts of devotion, he is a

The agora in Philippi. This site was a busy marketplace when Paul arrived first at Philippi in A.D. 49.

prize winner. He was circumcised as an eight-day-old baby. He was no last minute convert, but as a baby his parents had obediently fulfilled the command God gave Abraham in Genesis 17:12.

In addition, Paul writes, he is not only a Jew; he is the best kind—a member of David's family. And to cap it off, he wasn't a Sadducee, with a non-nationalistic record of compromise and duplicity with the hated Roman conquerors, he was a Pharisee. This was an important distinction to his Jewish or Jewish-taught readers (3:5).

The Pharisees were members of a lay movement that began during the time of Judas Maccabaeus, who in 166 B.C. succeeded his father as leader in the fight for Jewish independence from Syria. The Pharisees became the most sincere and devout believers in Judaism, and Paul had been a proud member of this select group.

He next adds, "Concerning zeal, persecuting the church; touching the righteousness which is in the law, blameless" (3:6). Paul's zeal as Saul of Tarsus in attempting to stamp out the early "followers of the Way" had been widely known, and he was a feared man in the early days of the young Church. Luke wrote of this young terrorist that he breathed "out threatenings and slaughter against the disciples of the Lord" (Acts 9:1). Indeed, from his point of reference in those early days as a Pharisee, Paul had been blameless.

Now, as Paul continues his personal odyssey, he touches on the shocking reversal that fundamentally changed his whole life (3:7–11). Actually, it was a series of key, journeying event-moments, which probably began quite early, when he was a student of Rabbi Gamaliel. Doubtless a most important event-moment in this chain was his participation in the death of Stephen. During that time his apparent inner struggle against the tugging of God drove him from one violent act to another.

A Dramatic Change.

But then Paul's event-moments took him in a different direction: He met the Lord on the road to Damascus, and his lost eyesight was tenderly restored in the little house of Ananias. From there he went into seclusion for a time, and at the right moment Barnabas found him in Tarsus and solicited his help for work in the church at Antioch (Acts 11:22–26).

What an amazing series of beginnings for Paul's spiritual story. But this, of course, was only the beginning of his spiritual event-moments, as we saw in our studies of Acts. While most of us may not have a record of hate and violence in our lives, the experience of God at work in us is also a series of event-moments. The miracle of God's grace is awesome!

A Study in Contrasts.   Paul now creates a series of superlative contrasts (3:8–9), which includes one that even by first-century standards would be considered a crude literary expletive. The King James text reads, "…for whom I have suffered the loss of all things, and do count them but *dung*, that I may win Christ"(3:8, italics mine). Other versions translate the word "dung" as refuse, garbage, or rubbish.

Actually, the Greek word Paul used in the writing of this particular contrast denoted two things in his day: (1) human excrement, and (2) the refuse or leavings from a feast. It seems to me the point Paul is making here is that "refuse" or "garbage" or "rubbish" is food rejected for not having nutritive qualities. His intention, then, in using this surprising word, is to say that before he met Christ on the Damascus road, none of his legalistic achievements in the Jewish religion had provided real food to nourish his life. He had not received life-nourishment until he accepted Christ as Savior and Lord.

This is not to say that Paul has rejected the Law as God's Law, but he has rejected the confidence that he used to have in himself as being righteous on his own. He was rejecting any thought of achieving righteousness based on his accomplishments in following the Law. Justification, or being made right before God, has come through fulfillment of the Law in Christ, and the life-nourishment that everyone searches for comes only from the Lord of the Law.

In other words, in verse 9 Paul is emphasizing that he has no righteousness of his own based on the Law. Any such "righteousness" would merely be refuse or garbage or dung.

We know from what Paul has written in Romans and Galatians that the Law can bring us or lead us to Christ, and like a holy mirror it faithfully shows us how we really look—it can reveal but not heal or cleanse what it discloses. For Paul, it was not his own righteousness that made him right with God, but faith—trusting in the faithfulness of God. Faith was the "means," not the "source" of being made right.

Paul now shares his primary goal in life, "That I may know him, and the power of his resurrection, and the fellowship of his sufferings, being made conformable unto his death" (3:10). The Christian faith is not an impersonal ledger entry made in heaven; it is a relationship with Christ *here and now*.

And this relationship is possible through "the power of his resurrection." The power in the Christian's life is the power of the resurrection of Jesus— the defeat of death. And this defeat is not only a spiritual victory, it is also a victory of the body over death— the whole self is vindicated by Christ's resurrection.

Paul says something else in verse 10 that is highly significant when he speaks of "the fellowship of his sufferings." This might be better translated "share his sufferings." Once again the word *koinonia* comes up. This is the word Paul uses for "fellowship" or "share." I believe what Paul is expressing here is that he wants to be as totally identified with Christ as possible in His suffering and death and in His victory over death.

We get from this, I believe, a statement of Paul's own discovery that Jesus is the Lord who *can be known personally*. No greater Good News could come to us than this— *we can know Christ personally*! You have heard that before, as I have. In fact, we've heard it so often, it may have lost its power. But after seeing Jesus Christ through Paul's eyes as he has written to the Christians in Philippi, this power-packed truth becomes amazingly fresh and new.

Paul Looks to the Future.

The great apostle to the Philippian Christians has been writing with passion. But he doesn't ease up as he continues (3:12–14). His language in these verses takes on an athletic tone. The picture seems to be of a runner looking ahead toward the goal— the final tape at the end of the race.

As he looks ahead, he readily admits to not being perfect. The word translated "perfect" in verse 12 actually means "complete" or "at the goal." Some versions have translated it as "mature." Paul is fully aware of his own inadequacy, his own shortcomings in the race of life, but he assures his readers that he is in the race, he is pressing on.

Three times in verse 12 Paul uses a word that means "to take," "to apprehend." His Greek readers would not have missed this unique play on words, which I have translated this way: "I have not already *apprehended* the goal ...but I race to *apprehend* it...because Christ has *apprehended* me." In this we see that Paul's motivation for everything he does in life has its origin in the Good News of Christ's love. His motivation for the life-race is not fear or guilt or pride. Rather, it is his enthusiastic acceptance of the Lord.

The Good News for all of us is that we don't strain in the race to make God's team; we're already on it! The challenge for us as we live the Christian life comes from Christ's love for us. And in that love we have the assurance that Jesus is with us before the race, during the race, and after the race.

In verse 13 Paul readily admits that he hasn't made it so far on his own, but then he goes on to add, "But this one thing I do." There was nothing fragmented about his objective; his priorities were in order, and his focus was sharp. He then brings into play three verb tenses that describe any life pilgrimage: the past, the present, and the future, and he uses three verbs in these verses that relate to each of the three tenses— the past— "*forgetting* those things which are behind"; the future—"*reaching forth* unto those things which are before"; the present—"I *press* toward the mark for the prize of the high calling of God in Christ Jesus" (3:13–14).

Paul knew well the importance of forgetting the past. As a persecutor and hater of Christians before his confrontation with the Lord on the Damascus road, he knew the importance of forgetting those infamous years. He knew that a runner doesn't look back over his shoulder. To do so is to lose the rhythm of the race.

On July 27, 1985, Steve Cram of Great Britain set a new world record for the mile at Oslo, Norway. He ran it in 3 minutes, 46.31 seconds, breaking the 1981 record of Sebastian Coe. As I watched that spectacular race, I was impressed by Cram's focused discipline as he held his lead position. Only once did he even slightly turn to look for Coe and Gonzalez, who were following him. To look back could have caused him to lose his stride and might have cost him the race.

As Paul sees it, the Christian lives in the present, from the past, and for the future, but the past does not mortgage the alive possibilities of the present. In writing as he

Scattered ruins and columns of churches in Philippi. Just ten miles inland from the port city of Neapolis on the Egnatian road, Philippi was a major Roman center in the first century.

does, it is clear that Paul remembers the past experiences of his life, for he knows they are an important part of who he is. But in a most practical way he never lets what has happened take his eyes away from future goals.

Paul now urges his readers to think carefully about all he has written here about the pilgrimage toward spiritual maturity—and "be thus minded" (3:15). The reference here is not to a mental state, but to a focused and definite

A Thoughtful Pattern for Life.

way of thinking. This is a tremendously energetic idea; it involves the hard work of thorough and careful thinking.

This is a remarkable verse. Throughout this letter Paul has given his readers a vigorous description of a pattern of life that is right for him in his journey with Christ. But now he asks them to think carefully through their own patterns—they are to seek their own spiritual guidance. He avoids any form of oppressive paternalism or manipulation.

As he has done so often before, Paul models an important principle for us. It is terribly tempting in our relationships with family and other Christians to think their Christian pilgrimage should be exactly the same as ours. So often we are critical of others for not being at the same point of spiritual maturity—or immaturity—that we are. But Paul was too wise to fall into that trap. Instead, he gave his own witness and shared with others what he felt was right for his life and then he committed them to the Lord. Paul wasn't guilty of playing God, nor should we be.

Learn by Imitation.

Paul now gives his friends some extremely practical advice that applies to what he has been telling them (3:17). When he writes, "Brethren, be followers together of me, and mark them which walk so as ye have us for an ensample," he is actually suggesting that they imitate him, that they follow his example.

I do not see this to be a contradiction of what we discussed in the previous section. I don't believe he is setting down a hard-and-fast rule for everyone to live exactly as he does. But he does seem to be suggesting that they imitate him in spirit and attitude.

Paul's judgment is extremely sound, for we learn by watching others. Johann Sebastian Bach watched and listened carefully to the great organist-composer Dietrich Buxtehude, and that experience greatly shaped the man who would then become an even greater genius than his mentor.

A skier learns to ski by watching a teacher-skier and then imitating the teacher's actions on the learning slopes. We learn by watching experts and then adapting their approach into our own style. And in a similar way we grow and mature in our discipleship by learning from our mentors and models in the Lord.

As he draws this section to a close, Paul turns his attention once again to those "enemies of the cross of Christ" (3:18). I believe his reference here is to those legalists who were demanding that the Philippians be obedient to the Jewish Law, including the rite of circumcision.

He continues to stand firmly against this. Paul understands the danger in substituting a physical act of religious devotion for the centrality of Jesus Christ. Salvation comes by faith in Christ alone, not by performing religious acts, no matter how good they might be.

It is also possible that Paul may have had in mind the danger posed by incipient Gnosticism. This was another false way which was also "an enemy of the cross." Gnostics believed that the physical body was of no importance since the Christian had a mystical spiritual relationship with Christ that was assured by secret knowledge. This simply meant that since the Christian has been accepted by Christ, personal actions didn't matter.

An Important Warning.

Paul's central challenge in verses 18 and 19 is, "If the shoe fits, put it on." Then he moves on to a grand design statement of the positive affirmation of the gospel of Christ. In verse 20 Paul writes, "For our conversation is in heaven." Some versions translate "conversation" as "commonwealth." Literally it means that our "citizenship" is in heaven. Put another way, "We are citizens of heaven!"

Earlier in this letter Paul had encouraged the Christians in Philippi to be real people in a real world and witness to their faith by words and actions. He builds now on that idea by saying that it is possible for them to live as productive Christians in Philippi because in a very profound sense their citizenship is in heaven.

In other words, we live Christian lives in the real present, with specific street addresses and political and social realities, but the completion of God's gift to us is that at the same time *we are citizens of heaven.* And we live in sure expectation of the return of Jesus Christ. This present world belongs to God, and when Christ returns He will transform our bodies to become what He wants them to be. Such being the case, any religious physical acts like circumcision are not necessary for us to be acceptable to God.

The Christian's Citizenship.

And, on the other hand, for those who might be tempted by the heresy of Gnosticism, the strongest argument against that teaching is the importance Christ places on our bodies. He will "change our vile body, that it may be fashioned like unto his glorious body" (3:21).

The whole point of our hope of resurrection is that it is our *whole* self that is loved by Christ. Our whole self—our emotions, our personalities, our distinctive characteristics—the total mixture of all that we are is loved by Jesus Christ. In Christ, we are important to God!

Father God, Help me to live with an eternal perspective on things—help me to know in a life-changing way that I am a sojourner here. I am privileged to be a citizen of Your Kingdom. Amen.

WHAT THIS SCRIPTURE MEANS TO ME—Philippians 3

When our son graduated from high school, friends and relatives sent him graduation gifts. In the days after graduation I suggested more than once that he really needed to write thank-you letters for the gifts. "Yes, Mother," he'd say, "you've already told me." To which I replied, "Yes, but you haven't written yet. When you write, I'll stop reminding you."

Mothers are often accused of nagging, but Paul must have felt the same necessity to remind his Philippian friends when he was writing again to them about some very important matters. In this lesson he warns them about two extremes in Christianity—legalism and license.

In a city where we once lived, there was a church that attracted quite a large congregation. All of the Bible classes were conducted by the pastor because he wouldn't trust anyone else to do the teaching. We could soon see that the kind of people who were attracted to the church were those who wanted hard and fast lines drawn as to what was "Christian" and what wasn't. They wanted simple answers to complex questions.

The church developed a very rigid creed, and as long as the members followed it and attended every service, they believed they were good Christians. But somehow none of them seemed to be very happy about it all. A critic said, "Their faces look as if their shoes are pinching them." And a former member commented, "They know a lot about what the Bible says, but not much about Christian love." Their attitude was a strong reminder to me to guard against stern legalism.

The other extreme is license. My husband and I were greatly saddened when a talented young minister friend of ours was forced to resign from his church because of personal improprieties. His wife divorced him because of his involvement with other women, and the church was deeply shocked by his misbehavior. He hurt his family, the church, his friends, and the cause of Christ because of his failure to apply the Good News of Christ to his personal life.

Neither legalism nor license brings joy in the Christian faith. Instead, Paul has urged us to choose the right goal—a maturing relationship with Jesus Christ. Paul gave us some excellent advice in our lesson about focusing on the right goal "...forgetting those things which are behind, and reaching forth unto those things which are before" (3:13). In the Los Angeles Olympic games a runner made the mistake of looking over his shoulder to see how close the next runner was, and that one look threw him off stride and he lost the race. Paul's advice was to forget what is behind and always look ahead.

As a young girl growing up, I had several different models. My mother modeled the role of a Christian wife and mother. A teacher modeled a woman's quest for excellence in learning. An aunt's hospitality modeled the art of making others feel welcome in our home.

But Paul's attitude toward Christ gives us a model for all of life, "I press toward the mark for the prize of the high calling of God in Christ Jesus" (3:14).

LESSON 4
PHILIPPIANS 4

Farewell Instructions

Savior, Daily I am assaulted by the way and temptations of this world. Compromise, disobedience, and sin are at every turn. Lord, help me to not be moved by difficulties, disappointments, or strange winds of doctrine. Help me to "stand fast" in You—be my anchor, my stay. AMEN.

Hold Steady in the Lord. Paul opens this last part of the letter to his beloved friends at Philippi with words that express his deep feelings for them, even as he urges them to hold steady. Earlier in his letter he had urged them to "stand fast in one spirit" (1:27). Now he is telling them "to stand fast in the Lord" (4:1).

Based on his original Greek wording, Paul seems to be suggesting that they are to dig in like soldiers and never give an inch, irrespective of the opposition they face. We don't know all the problems that were disturbing the Christians and the church at Philippi or the pressures that were closing in on them because of their faith. But Paul is urging them to stand firm in their faith—to dig in—and not compromise.

As is so typical of Paul, however, he precedes the "hold steady" instruction with a grand affirmation of love for them. Once again we are privileged to look deeply into

Paul's heart as he expresses his keenly felt love and affection for his friends. And, once again, we can learn from him as he unabashedly puts his feelings into words.

He uses four words here to express the depth and warmth of his feelings. In referring to them as "dearly beloved," he uses a form of *agape*, one of his favorite terms, which he used twenty-seven times in his writings to his Christian friends. Most certainly there was nothing casual or superficial about his expression of love. Paul didn't use this word lightly, as we sometimes do—"I just love your new car" or "I love the way that red dress looks on you." For Paul, the word *love* carried a deep and profound meaning.

The second word that expresses his feelings for them is translated "and longed for." Unlike *agape*, this was not a word Paul used a great deal. In fact, the root word for this expression appears only five times in all his writings (Phil. 1:8 and 2:26, 2 Cor. 9:14, and Rom. 15:23). We get the feeling here that Paul is "homesick" for them.

Third, Paul speaks of his friends as being "my joy." This particular expression is used many times in this letter. Over and over again he reminds his readers that they are a source of great joy to him. They are his friends, and even though their life journey is marked with times of failure, they are still "his joy."

And finally, Paul refers to them as his "crown." For the Greeks, the kind of crown referred to here was worn in victory—for celebration. It was not the kind of crown that would be worn by an emperor or king, but was rather like a victory wreath worn by a returning soldier or champion athlete. In effect Paul is telling them here that they are his celebration wreath.

What a marvelous commentary Paul has given us of the attitude we should have toward our Christian brothers and sisters. Remember, Paul's Philippian readers were Christians, "warts and all." The church in Philippi wasn't perfect, and the Christians who belonged to that church weren't perfect either. But they loved Paul and he loved them. And as we see here, he was able to tell them how he felt. I'm sure there are those around us in church every Sunday who are starved to know that we care, that we love them, that they are a joy to us, and that our relationship is cause for celebration.

Healing Differences.

We are next introduced briefly to three people: Euodias, Syntyche, and Clement (4:2–3). We know nothing more about Euodias and Syntyche than what is written here. These were common names in first-century society, and it is likely they were prominent members of the church. Clement was also a rather common name in the first century; however, Origen and Eusebius, early church fathers, believed that this Clement later became the bishop at Rome and was the author of the letter of Clement to the Corinthians (A.D. 110–120).

The one thing we can be sure of is that these people were involved in a quarrel that sorely disturbed Paul. At least Euodias and Syntyche were quarreling, and it isn't clear whether Clement was part of the problem or whether he was one of the "true yokefellows" trying to settle the dispute.

Without giving us the cause for the quarrel, Paul does take us behind the scenes a bit. This brief mention deserves our attention, I believe, not so much because of those who were quarreling but because of Paul's attitude. He doesn't seem to question their motives or their Christianity, and he doesn't take sides. Rather, he approaches the problem as a sensitive Christian friend and pastor-counselor. Notice what Paul says and what he does not say.

Not only does he not take sides, he doesn't write up a list of things that may have caused the quarrel. He doesn't threaten or scold any of the people involved, and he doesn't suggest any disciplinary action the church should use against those creating the disturbance.

But he does admit there is a quarrel, and he names in a forthright manner the people involved. Then Paul calls on them to find a place of agreement in the Lord. In other words, even though there may be points of difference between them, they are to find common ground—those places of agreement in Christ—and build their fellowship around those. There is a very profound meaning in this idea. As Christians, our relationships with one another are not to be viewed as being independent of our faith. Rather, they are all to be viewed in relationship to Christ and our faith.

Regardless of the differences of opinion that may honestly trouble us in our relationships with other Christians

All that is left of what was a large library in Philippi.

and within our church life, we are to find a way to stand together in Christ and creatively try to work through secondary points of disagreement.

Peter and Paul beautifully illustrated this approach toward interpersonal and doctrinal disagreements in their Antioch encounter (see Gal. 2 and Acts 15). They found their most basic and common footing in the all-sufficiency of Christ, and then they were able to work through to a satisfactory resolution on other matters. There is no suggestion in any of this that when differences of opinion and interpretation arise *within* the Christian fellowship we are to go on the personal attack and begin to draw lines that separate "right" from "wrong" for everyone else. Instead, Paul's sensitive reactions are based on the attitudes of love and appreciation he expressed in verse 1, the "high road" that can sustain unity while allowing for differences.

Paul then goes on to solicit help from the "true yoke-fellow," in resolving the difficulty (4:3). The original meaning of this phrase to Paul and his readers would have been "true comrade" or "genuine comrade." There is no specific identification of the yokefellow, but it may have been an individual person or the church acting as a group. But the point being made is simply this: The people who were quarreling were to be helped—they were to be lifted up. They were not to be ostracized, but *helped*!

One thing further is added in verse 3 for the benefit of the "yokefellow" who was to help resolve the quarrel. Paul reminds him, or them, that Euodias and Syntyche and Clement "laboured with me in the gospel,...and with other my fellowlabourers, whose names are in the book of life." They had been and still were Paul's colleagues. Paul doesn't want them put down because of their problem; instead, they are to be respected and not scorned.

At the same time Paul reminds his readers that the names of those who were quarreling "are in the book of life." We know from this and other such references in the New Testament that these people were accepted and loved by the Lord. Having that information would certainly guide the helper or helpers not to be either patronizing or self-righteous.

Rejoice in the Lord—
a Christian Quality.

This is the second time within the space of a few words that Paul has urged his readers to "rejoice in the Lord" (3:1, 4:4). But now he gives it a double emphasis as he writes, "Rejoice in the Lord alway: and again I say, Rejoice."

The exuberance of this great sentence of Paul has been one of the wonderful gifts to Christians of all time, and it certainly must have greatly encouraged the church at Philippi. After all, Paul was in serious trouble, but he could urge them to be full of joy. At the same time they were having their share of problems. From the Jewish side of their fellowship, questions of legalism and Law were creating dissension. From the Greek side, Gnosticism was contaminating the church. And now certain of their leaders were quarreling. It was a kind of "doom-and-gloom" situation—the kind confirmed pessimists really enjoy.

But from the confines of Nero's prison Paul tells them twice in one sentence to rejoice in the Lord. There were to be no feelings of defeat. And certainly there was to be no giving in to the forces that would divide them and minimize their witness.

In addition to being full of joy, Paul now urges his readers to be moderate (4:5). The particular word he used here is virtually impossible to translate into English, but it seems to carry connotations of openness, moderation, gentleness. Its other uses in the New Testament help us see how different writers understood the word: in 1 Peter 2:18 "...not only to the good and gentle"; and in James 3:17, "But the wisdom that is from above is first pure, then peaceable, gentle...."

Paul here models a fascinating mixture of enthusiastic shouts of joy and the inner and interpersonal quality of moderateness, mellowness. And he adds that all of this is possible because, "The Lord is at hand." We know that the Lord is with us now and that the day is coming when He will return in triumph.

Jesus Christ will resolve history at its ending, just as He stands at history's beginning—even as He is history's radical center. He makes the real difference in all of life. This is the basis for our joy, irrespective of the conditions that surround us.

Now Paul moves to assure his readers that even in the face of certain outward conditions they are to "Be careful for nothing" (4:6)—they are not to be anxious or feel harassed. Peter used the same word Paul does here when he wrote, "Casting all your care upon him; for he careth for you" (1 Peter 5:7)—put all of your anxieties on Jesus because He cares for you. And Jesus used the same word in the Sermon on the Mount when He said, "Take therefore no thought for the morrow" (Matt. 6:34)—don't be anxious about what may happen tomorrow.

Then Paul goes on in verse 6 to say, "but in every thing by prayer and supplication with thanksgiving let your

*Moderation and Gentleness—
Christian Qualities.*

Peace through Prayer.

requests be made known unto God." Here, Paul is encouraging the Christians at Philippi to challenge the real harassment of continuous and low-grade fear by bringing their whole selves along with their requests to the Lord. It is rather interesting that the Greek word translated "pray" in the New Testament should actually read "pray toward." From this we come to understand that biblical prayer is focused primarily upon or toward the One to whom we pray rather than upon the act or practice of prayer.

When praying, Paul continues, we are to be *specific* in making our requests known to God. Prayer in the Bible is the specific and definite thinking of things through before God. That is exactly what Paul encourages his readers to do.

We are invited by our Friend Jesus Christ in the "Our Father" prayer to bring the requests and real concerns of our daily lives, including our need for food, to the Father in prayer. Now Paul reminds his readers of all time of that generous invitation.

But our requests are to be made "with thanksgiving." The idea conveyed here by Paul in the Greek word he used is that our thanksgiving is the "good joy" we offer to God in all things.

Paul then shows us the outcome of such prayer, "And the peace of God, which passeth all understanding, shall keep your hearts and minds through Christ Jesus" (4:7). The peace that belongs to God is His to give, and it is a peace that has within it the sense of wholeness and health. The literal meaning of what Paul is saying is that God's peace is able to guard our hearts and minds from the pressures that cause fear and harassment.

Think on These Things.

In our lesson so far, Paul has told his Philippian friends that they should empty their minds of fear and anxiety and anything else that will detract from their faith pilgrimage. Now, he gives them a list of virtues they should think about and meditate on (4:8–9). Paul's selection of the eight virtues mentioned in the eighth verse should not be seen as an attempt to list all possible virtues. Rather, we have here examples of the kinds of things that should fill our minds: that which is true, honest, just, pure, lovely, and whatever is of good report or is excellent. Wise people for thousands of years have expressed the idea that we are what we think about. Let us think prayerfully and

Tradition holds that this is the entry way to Paul's prison in Philippi (Acts 16:23). It was here, after the earthquake, that the jailer and his entire family were saved.

A view of the ruins of a small theater and the surrounding countryside in Philippi.

thoughtfully on virtues of the kind Paul has listed here, and with God's help these will become a natural part of our day-to-day living.

Paul then follows the virtue-packed sentence with a challenge to action: "Those things, which ye have both learned, and received, and heard, and seen in me, do: and the God of peace shall be with you" (4:9). We are to focus all our energies on *being* and *doing*. First, our minds are to be flooded with Christian virtues; then we are to act; to be, to do. The Christian faith, for Paul, is both thoughtful because it is grounded in Jesus Christ, who is the truth, and it is active because it involves journeying with Christ who is alive and active Himself.

A Special Gift from God.

In verse 10 Paul expresses his appreciation for the Philippians' faithfulness in tracking him down. Apparently they had been out of touch for a time during his trials and imprisonment in Jerusalem and Caesarea and on his long ship journey to Rome. He wants them to be reassured, though, that he is glad they've found him and that he is not discouraged or discontented.

Paul then gave his Philippian friends, and us, what is possibly the greatest affirmation to be found anywhere in his writings, "I can do all things through Christ which strengtheneth me" (4:13). Paul is saying here that because of the massive infusion of God's power he is equal to anything and everything that might come his way. And the great Good News for each of us is that *in Christ* we can make it!

Partnership through Generosity.

Now as Paul comes to the final words of this love letter to his beloved friends in Philippi, he expresses his deeply felt appreciation for the way they have always shared with him in his difficult and troubled times (4:14). Their love and friendship dates back to his first visit to Philippi, and they have always been supportive of him. He even recalls in verses 15 and 16 the time years before when they had sent help to him while he was getting the church started in the Macedonian capital of Thessalonica. And then he reminds them that not only had their gifts been a great help to him, but they themselves had been especially blessed as well, and God had been pleased.

The point being made in verse 18 is that although God doesn't require sacrifices as an atonement for our sins, He does accept our gifts of concern and involvement as a sacrifice pleasing to Him. This means that the love that overflows from our life in Christ becomes the fulfillment in the New Covenant of the ancient Hebrew rites of sacrifice as described in the Old Testament.

Next comes another of Paul's great affirmations in which he assures them and us that we cannot outgive God: "But my God shall supply all your need according to his riches in glory by Christ Jesus" (4:19). There can be no doubt but that Paul wrote those words with the greatest of conviction. He had traveled thousands of long and hard miles under extremely difficult and trying circumstances. Many times over the years he had been in hostile territory without friends to help him. But through it all God had supplied every need he had. Now, even though he was confined in a Roman prison, God's supply line was not cut off. His every need was being met.

And now, before his concluding "Amen," he voices once again his praise to the Lord, "Now unto God and our Father be glory for ever and ever. Amen" (4:20). Paul sees nothing from his prison cell but the glory and trustworthiness of God. His hymn of praise as he closes out the dictation to his close friends catches the spirit of the psalmist in Psalm 150. I suggest that before finishing this lesson you stop a moment and read those glory-filled six verses of Psalm 150 that form a grand benediction for our collection of Psalms.

Paul's Final Personal Words. As he has done with certain other letters, after concluding his dictation Paul now picks up a writing instrument and adds final lines of greeting in his own handwriting. In addition, he sends greetings from the "saints" in Rome who want to be remembered to the Christians in Philippi. And to that he adds an electrifying line, "...Chiefly they that are of Caesar's household" (4:22).

This added note tells us that even then there were Christians in high places. These may have been members of the Praetorian Guards. Or there has been strong speculation that Paul, during his final imprisonment, had been visited by Roman officials who were troubled and intrigued by this new Christian message that was penetrating Rome at the peak of its decadence under Emperor Nero.

There are accounts from early church writers that tell of visits between Paul and Seneca, the first-century Roman historian and writer. Seneca was the brother of Gallio, the Roman proconsul at Corinth when Paul was there. There is also mention in those same accounts of visits between Paul and Suetonius, the Roman historian.

Finally, Paul mentions the One greater than all others who shares his cell as he gives his final benediction to his readers, "The surprise love gift of the Lord Jesus Christ be with your spirit" (4:23, author's translation). Paul's every wish for his readers of all time is that they share personally with him the love of Christ. And while as far as he knew, he was writing only to his beloved friends who were living in Philippi during the first century, Paul's message is as fresh and up-to-date for us in the twentieth century as it was then.

Master, Thank You for Your "surprise love gift"—Jesus Christ the Messiah! AMEN.

WHAT THIS SCRIPTURE MEANS TO ME—Philippians 4

When I was a child attending vacation Bible school in South Georgia, we were given Scripture verses written on cards to memorize. Several of those Scriptures are still my favorites and some of them are found in Philippians. One of these is Philippians 4:8. On the card, it was written out almost like poetry,

> Finally, brethren,
> whatsoever things are true,
> whatsoever things are honest,
> whatsoever things are just,
> whatsoever things are pure,
> whatsoever things are lovely,
> whatsoever things are of good report;
> if there be any virtue, and if there be any praise,
> think on these things.

That was a hard verse for me to learn, but as a new Christian I really tried to remember it. And I'm glad I did because current studies show that Paul was ahead of his time. We now know that what a person reads, hears, watches on television, and thinks has a profound effect on his or her actions.

And then over the years as I have faced difficulties, I've repeated these words of Paul, "I can do all things through Christ which strengtheneth me" (4:13). As a teenager, when I was tempted to drift with the crowd, this verse reminded me that Christ would give me courage. As a young woman, with my first job in another state, it helped me face the challenges. As a wife and mother, I've been able to cope with the demands of everyday living with these words of Paul ringing in my ears. As I had to move and make adjustments through the years, it was this verse that reminded me I didn't have to do it alone. And as an older woman, I find the promise that Christ will strengthen me increasingly helpful.

Hanging over the desk where I sit to pay our bills is a small scroll with another verse from this chapter that is meaningful to me, "But my God shall supply all your need according to his riches in glory by Christ Jesus" (4:19). My husband and I claimed this verse when we were newlyweds and made the decision to follow God's will for our lives.

Because Ken felt called to be a minister, we knew that where God wanted him to serve would always be more important to us than what his salary was. But we also knew that we would have bills to pay just like everyone else. We realized the verse said *need* and not *want*—and there is a big difference between the two. So we asked God to help us to differentiate between *wants* and *needs* in our lives, and to guide us in our use of the money we had. We have found He has truly supplied all our needs—and many of our wants as well.

At the end of this letter, Paul again thanked the Philippians for their gifts. As Christians we are so frequently reminded to "love as Jesus loved" and to "give as Jesus gave" that it is sometimes more difficult for us to accept a gift of love than it is to give one. It may have been this way with Paul, also. He was so fiercely independent that it must have been hard for him to be on the receiving end.

I have frequently found it easier to give than to receive, too. While reflecting on this lesson, I was reminded of the time many years ago when I was trying hard to get acquainted with some new neighbors. I'd done all the nice things I could think of to do for them, but there was only polite coolness between us. Then my small child became quite ill, and to my surprise, one neighbor offered to take care of my baby while I took the sick child to the doctor. I would never have asked her, but I needed help and gratefully accepted. From then on we had a good relationship. I'd let her do some of the giving and had not insisted on being the only giver.

If someone is to have the joy of giving, there must be someone else who is willing to receive the gift in love. Paul said that the Philippian's gift not only helped him, but it also blessed those who gave it. And he reminded them that their gift was also a pleasing offering to God. After all, giving to others is actually our only way of giving to God!

Publisher's Introduction—Colossians

Geographically, our scene shifts dramatically from the city of Philippi in Northeast Greece (Macedonia) to a point in Asia Minor, roughly one hundred miles east of Ephesus in the Valley of the River Lycus. It was here, within just a few miles of each other, that the cities of Colossae, Hierapolis, and Laodicea were located. And it was to these Christians that Paul's letter to the Colossians was written.

While Paul had neither founded nor visited these churches, he felt a close relationship with them because undoubtedly they were a mission outgrowth of the church at Ephesus where he had spent three years in ministry. Indirectly, at least, these young Christians were his children in the Lord.

As with all of the young churches of that time, the Colossian Christians were just a short step from the pagan practices and worship that had been so much a part of their earlier life. There had been little opportunity for the kind of teaching that firmly establishes Christians in their faith. For this reason they needed all the encouragement and advice they could get.

In this perceptive letter, Paul models for Christians of all time the important ministry of encouragement. With remarkable insight, tact and sincerity, he affirms their worth and accomplishments in the Lord. Then he moves on to speak out firmly on what has come to be known as the Colossian heresy. There is a considerable difference of opinion as to what this was, but from the content of the letter it would appear to be an odd mixture of Jewish legalism and Greek spiritualism.

On the one hand, there were evidently those who claimed to be super-saints because they observed certain Jewish practices like circumcision. And on the other hand, there were those that laid stress on a kind of secret knowledge that came through a special revelation. Both of these false teachings diluted the simple gospel message and turned the focus away from Jesus Christ as the supreme Center of our faith. As would be expected, these "strange voices" were causing considerable confusion and disunity among the Christians.

To counteract this false teaching, Paul turns the spotlight of his instruction on the person of Christ and His relationship to the real world in which we live. Paul's opposition in the Lycus Valley focused on an otherwordly asceticism. And so Paul first establishes a solid foundation in a flesh-and-blood Jesus of Nazareth who died for the sins of the human race but was raised bodily on the third day in resurrection glory. Then he comes down firmly on the practical application of a simple faith in the resurrected Lord in everyday relations—family life, vocation, the fellowship of the church, and life in society.

Although this letter was written well over nineteen hundred years ago to an obscure group of Christians in the Roman province of Asia, the wise counsel and helpful teaching it contains has particular relevance to the late twentieth-century Christian. We too are very much a part of a world that is searching for meaning in human relationships—marriage and family, parents and children, employer and employee. And while the shape of these relationships has changed considerably in our modern technological society, the substances of those relationships remain the same.

Preface to Colossians

There were three cities in Asia Minor, the region occupied by modern-day Turkey, that were located quite close to each other in the Valley of the Lycus—Laodicea, Hierapolis, and Colossae. The most important of the three was Laodicea, a very prosperous city in the first century. The ruins of its public buildings are a twentieth-century reminder of the city's past glory.

Seven miles from Laodicea, on the opposite side of the Lycus River, was the city of Hierapolis. Extensive ruins mark its location for today's inquisitive traveler.

And ten miles from Hierapolis stood the city of Colossae. Unfortunately, very little remains of this once important city. History records a visit at Colossae by Xerxes when he stopped off on his march against Greece. And even earlier, Cyrus, the founder of the Persian Empire, visited Colossae—one of his party described Colossae as "a populous city, prosperous and great."

But by the time of the first century, Colossae was a small town, overshadowed by the other two cities. It seems quite likely that it was the least important church that Paul wrote to. And we have no written record that the Apostle ever visited Colossae. In fact, by the wording of the letter we get the feeling that his knowledge of the church came pretty much from others, primarily Epaphras, a Colossian by birth and Paul's friend.

A logical question under these circumstances might well be, "Why did Paul, while he was in prison in Rome, write a letter to this small church in faraway Asia Minor?" The answer stems from a visit by Epaphras to Paul in Rome in which he shared his concern for the Colossian Christians and the problems confronting their church.

Then, too, Paul had gotten to know Onesimus, a young convert, who had escaped from his master, Philemon, who was Paul's friend and lived in Colossae. As a matter of fact, it is likely that Onesimus accompanied Tychicus on the trip from Rome when they personally delivered the Colossian letter and the one to Philemon. It is also possible that they carried and delivered the letter to the Ephesians at the same time.

The probable date for these letters is A.D. 63. This was undoubtedly toward the end of Paul's imprisonment and just a year before the great fire in Rome that triggered the most intense persecution of Christians up to that time.

What does this letter to the Colossian Christians have to say that is both helpful and important for us in the twentieth century? First, it communicates the Good News of Jesus Christ in a vigorous and positive way. Second, Paul skillfully and helpfully discusses two grave challenges that confronted those first-century Christians and that continue to be a problem today. Third, it offers some wise and ethical advice that can guide the behavior of Christians of every generation.

Finally, Colossians is an important letter for our study because of the added insight it gives us about the writer. The saga of the heart and mind of Paul continues to amaze us as we read on. And while this letter is set in real time, it is also a timeless part of the total witness of God's Word.

LESSON 5
COLOSSIANS 1

A Message for Young Christians

Everlasting Father, Thank You for Your wonderful gifts—Your salvation, Your Holy Spirit, Your written Word, Your peace, which passes all understanding. Help me to have an attitude of thanksgiving while I study this lesson. AMEN.

Following his usual practice, Paul opens this letter by identifying himself as an apostle of Jesus Christ and as the writer. At the same time he also identifies Timothy, his companion in Rome and "our brother" (1:1). And then in verse 2 he acknowledges specifically those to whom he is writing, "To the saints and faithful brethren in Christ which are at Colosse: Grace be unto you, and peace, from God our Father and the Lord Jesus Christ."

As we have seen from the Preface, Paul is writing this letter for the express purpose of dealing with certain specific problems that have arisen within their fellowship. However, he still refers to his readers as "saints and faithful brethren in Christ." In spite of what he had heard about their problems and questions, for Paul, they are still "in Christ," saints and brethren.

Next, Paul follows the custom of offering a prayer of thanksgiving for his readers. And even though he is fully aware of the problems he will be writing about shortly, he

Greeting and Expression of Thanksgiving.

expresses his appreciation for them and their faith (1:3–8). It is in the course of this expression of thanksgiving that we learn directly that it was Epaphras who first took the gospel to Colossae (1:7).

What little we know of Epaphras is found in three New Testament references: Colossians 1:7 and 4:12, and Philemon 23. A little later in this letter we get the definite impression that Epaphras had been sent by the churches in Colossae, Hierapolis, and Laodicea to be a special helper to Paul during his imprisonment in Rome. Then in Philemon 23 Paul refers to Epaphras as "my fellowprisoner in Christ Jesus." Apparently while Epaphras was in Rome he too was put in prison for his faith.

Early in this opening prayer, Paul thanks God for their *faith* in Christ, for their *love* for one another, and for their *hope*, the motivation for both their faith and love. For Paul, faith, hope, and love are basic to his understanding of the Christian faith (note 1 Cor. 13 and 1 Thess. 1:3). Their faith is anchored securely in the person of Jesus Christ; their love is the present-tense expression of good will toward one another in the fellowship of believers; and their hope is secure in God's future will for their lives.

Paul then does something that I'm sure must have been very encouraging to this small band of Christians in Colossae. He tells them that the Christian faith, which Epaphras had first introduced to them, is spreading and bearing fruit "in all the world" (1:6). Christians then and now need to know that our experiences of faith, hope, and love are not isolated happenings.

It is possible the church congregations in Colossae, Hierapolis, and Laodicea felt quite isolated and alone, located as they were about 100 miles inland from Ephesus. But now Paul assures them that they are not alone. Instead, they are part of a fellowship of faith that is growing as people come to know "the grace of God in truth." They were in fact a part of a worldwide fellowship of faith.

I'm sure it is likely that even in this day of instant news and speedy travel we sometimes feel alone and isolated. Our vision becomes narrowed because we see and are in contact with only our small group of Christian friends. At such moments we, too, need to be reminded as were Paul's readers that God has His people all across the world. On any given Sunday we can know that Christians of all races and languages are meeting together in worship and prayer—even those Christians who are forced to celebrate their love for the Lord in secret because of governmental oppression. No, we're never alone. We are not private Christians; rather, we belong to a fellowship that stretches across every barrier and boundary.

Paul now tells the Colossian Christians that since he heard of their "love in the Spirit," he does not cease to pray for them (1:9). As we read and reflect on Paul's writings in the New Testament, we come to understand that his prayers for people were intensely vigorous and thoughtful. Prayer was not a passive experience for him. As he concentrated on people and their needs, he prayed with an emotion-draining intensity.

Thoughtful Prayer.

We also learn from Paul's writings that he was the kind of person who kept track of people because he really cared for them. If we take his comments at face value, we must conclude that he prayed for many people on a regular basis. Undoubtedly, through Epaphras and others the Christians in Colossae had been told about Paul's faithfulness in prayer. So they must have been wonderfully reassured to know that they were a part of this vast circle of prayer.

I'm sure you've had the experience, as I have, of knowing that friends are praying for you. There have been times when the night of my life has seemed very dark and long, and yet I have gained strength because I knew in those very moments certain people were actively thinking about me and praying for me. When I visit with those friends in the Monday *agape* prayer group at our church and the Wednesday men's prayer group, it becomes clear to me that they know me in a deeper way than most other friends do because they have kept an appointment with the Lord in prayer for me. And during their times of prayer they have really focused their thoughts on me in a visual and active fashion.

That is what the word "intercession" means in the Old Testament—"to think through." And the Greek word translated "intercede" in the New Testament means to "carefully think through."

From Paul's words here I believe we get a much different picture of prayer than is common for must of us. To think carefully about those for whom we are praying, to actually see them on the screen of our minds, to visualize their needs, is to pray in the Spirit.

The Focus of Paul's Prayer for the Colossians.

Paul goes on in verses 9 and 10 to tell his readers what he is praying for. First he says that he prays they "might be filled with the knowledge of his will in all wisdom and spiritual understanding." Then he goes on to tell them that he prays such knowledge will cause them to lead lives that will be "fruitful" and pleasing to the Lord. In those two very descriptive verses Paul tells them that he prays both for their "thought life" and their lived-out "ethical life"— their day-to-day behavior.

Thought life and behavior, for Paul, are inseparable, and so he wants his Colossian readers to understand that what they "think" and what they "do" are one.

When Paul speaks of "wisdom" and "knowledge" and "understanding" in verse 9, he has used three words that conveyed a marvelous intensity to his Greek-speaking readers. The "knowledge" Paul speaks of here involves far more than a collection of information. Rather, it implies an expanding knowing of God's will and purpose. When he writes of "wisdom," the reference is to a quality of mental capability that reaches for the deepest of meanings. And the use of the word translated "understanding" carries the meaning of rare intelligence and insight, the facility of comprehension.

The Possible Colossian Problem.

At this point we might well ask why, at the very beginning of this letter, Paul has drawn on such rich imagery as he writes about knowing, wisdom, and insight. The most obvious reason may have been that they needed a filling up, an expansion of their knowledge. It is possible Paul felt they were really uninformed about their faith in its deepest sense.

But then a more complicated possibility exists. It might be that these Christians at Colossae had been taught by certain false teachers or leaders that special or even secret sources of wisdom, knowledge, and insight are available to those who are initiated into a special religious program being offered by these new teachers.

In other words, if the church at Colossae has indeed been invaded by teachers who advocate a cultic digression

A general view of the Hierapolis area. Hierapolis was the northernmost of the three cities located very close to each other in the Lycus Valley.

from the basic faith in Jesus that Epaphras had taught, Paul's challenge as he writes is much more difficult. And, if this is the case, Paul's letter might not be well accepted because these Lycus Valley Christians could be feeling the intoxication that comes from the idea that the "beginner Christian" has received superior and exotic insight from otherwise hidden sources. It is even possible that these new and false teachers may have used the very words Paul employed here to impress and promote their ideas.

If this understanding of what happened in Colossae is true, then Paul's readers would have been attracted right at the outset with his elegant vocabulary. And I happen to believe this interpretation of the Colossian situation is the most likely.

As we move ahead in our study of this letter, it becomes quite clear that the Colossian Christians are indeed entrapped to some degree in a form of Gnosticism that has both Jewish and Greek overtones. On the one hand, Paul is forced to cope with certain forms of Jewish legalism, and on the other hand, we see clear evidence of Greek dualism in which the body is rejected as the spirit is glorified. This particular aberration of the gospel message stressed that the Christian faith reached its noblest purpose and glory in a mystical spiritualism.

In attempting to assist these young Christians in regaining their sure footing and finding their true Living Center in the Lord Jesus, Paul is presented with a tremendous challenge. How could he be helpful to them and at the same time avoid a harsh defensiveness? That was a question that confronted not only Paul in the first century, but one that we must answer, as well-meaning people in our churches today become deluded by exotic teaching and are involved in religious movements that can be dangerous to the health of their new-found faith.

Paul's Response.   Paul prepared the way for his response before he even started to write this letter. He prayed for these young and endangered believers. Then he began his letter with a bold use of the very vocabulary that would speak to them. But as he writes, he makes it clear that the "knowledge" words that are so appealing to them are first of all captive to the Lordship of Christ—the highest knowledge is to know God (1:10). And at the same time, these very words are intimately involved with practical discipleship and Christian living, "That ye might walk worthy of the Lord."

In verse 11 Paul prays for God's mighty strength that these Christians may be courageous disciples of joy right there in the Lycus Valley. And in verse 12 he breaks into words of praise and thankfulness because God is the One who has "qualified" us to live as Christians in the light of God. Our King James text states it this way, "Giving thanks unto the Father, which hath made us meet [qualified] to be partakers of the inheritance of the saints in light."

The point Paul is making here is most important. We, of ourselves, irrespective of any knowledge and wisdom we may have, cannot do anything to qualify us or make us competent to be members of God's new society in Jesus Christ. It is God who has made this possible; He has qualified us. No wonder Paul broke out at this point with praise to God!

Paul closes this grand expression of thanksgiving (1:13–14) by focusing our attention on the *why* and *how* of our being heirs of God and joint heirs of Jesus Christ: God "hath delivered us." He has rescued us from the power, the authority, of darkness and made us His in Christ. And it is in Christ that we have "redemption"—freedom, pardon, release.

In this part of our lesson we see now that Paul has already begun the cure for the spiritual problem that has a foothold in the Colossian church by turning his readers' attention away from any specialized promises of power or secret knowledge. Instead, he has focused their attention on the true source of all knowledge, wisdom, and power—Jesus Christ.

Paul now zeroes in forcefully on the aberration that threatens to corrupt the church at Colossae. The Gnosticism that had invaded the thinking of these young Christians was an attempt to interpret Christianity as just another school of philosophy. Beginning with the Gnostic foundational idea that all forms of matter are evil, the teachers of Gnosticism assumed that the true God was not the creator because He wouldn't have had anything to do with evil. In addition, they had a low view of Jesus in terms of His unique role in the world, and at the same time they insisted that Jesus was not actually human, but a spirit with a body. Finally, these false teachers did not accept Jesus as the sole means of salvation.

The Gnostics dignified this fuzzy thinking by asserting that the only way a person could find God was through a mystical and secret kind of knowledge. This, of course, denied everything Paul stood for, and became what students have come to call the "Colossian heresy." In combating the foundational beliefs of the Gnostics, Paul now launches into one of his loftiest and most beautiful passages (1:15–20).

For Paul, everything he believes is focused on the Person of Jesus Christ who, he writes, "is the image of the

Jesus as the Creator.

85

invisible God, the firstborn of every creature" (1:15). The Greek word Paul uses here that is translated "image" has two distinct meanings. First, it means "representation"—for example, the imprint of Caesar's face on a coin. Second, it means a "manifestation"—showing the nature of an invisible reality. Paul's intention in this fifteenth verse is to include both ideas—Christ is the One who shows to us the nature of the invisible God. We can know God through His self-disclosure in Jesus Christ who is the firstborn of all creation.

Paul's use of "firstborn" may seem a bit puzzling at first. However, a study of such Old Testament references as Exodus 4:22 and Psalms 89:27 helps us to see that this is essentially a messianic term that has two principle meanings: 1) Christ has *priority* over all of creation; 2) Christ is *sovereign* over all creation.

Next, Paul adds, "For by him were all things created" (1:16). Paul is saying that Jesus is indeed the Creator. Admittedly, we're dealing with a rather complex concept here, but the important truth for Paul's readers in Colossae and for us now is that for the Apostle *Jesus is the complete revelation of God.*

Jesus Is Lord over All Powers.

Paul then builds his word picture of Jesus with a dramatic catalog of the most impressive power words in the Greek language—thrones, dominions, principalities, powers (1:16). Christ is indeed the co-author of these different kinds of powers and authorities. Paul was very familiar with the first-century preoccupation of many Jews and Gnostics with ranking in terms of importance the angels and spirits and powers. In fact, this idea seemed to intrigue many of the early church fathers.

But Paul has no time for such speculations. He concentrates on the basics and focuses his entire attention on Jesus Christ who was and is the Lord of all. It is true that his language here and elsewhere reflects his awareness of the presence in the world of different kinds of powers—good and bad, angelic and demonic. But he does not become sidetracked with any of this because he knows the One who is above and over all.

A friend of mine who is a pastor in the Philippines shared with me a very practical experience he had that brings into focus Paul's wisdom in writing to the Colossians as he did. There was a death in this young pastor's family; and he, along with other relatives, traveled to the family home in a rural province for the funeral. While there, he was confronted with certain local taboos practiced by some members of the family. They refused to disturb a certain room in the house for fear of offending the spirits of the dead man and other ancestors because of the bad luck such an intrusion might cause.

My young pastor friend realized that this fear was a hold-over from the old animistic traditions and was something his family needed to forsake; but in the spirit of Paul in writing to the Colossian Christians, he put first things first. He didn't deny the possibility of powers—spiritual or otherwise—that might affect human life. Instead, he claimed the greater authority of the Lord Jesus in whom his family trusted. He urged them to claim Christ's authority over all powers that might be present.

It is true that in our sophisticated culture most of us are free from the superstition that afflicted some in my pastor friend's family. However, we should not take lightly the forces of evil that are present in our world. At the same time, though, we are reminded by Paul here that our Lord is supreme. In Christ we can handle anything life has to offer.

Christ Holds Everything Together.

Paul continues his description of Christ in verse 17, "And he is before all things, and by him all things consist." Perhaps a better way to word this last phrase is, "In Him all things hold together, or cohere." In other words, the whole universe is held together by Jesus Christ! The root of the word Paul uses here appears in a fascinating sentence that he wrote to the Corinthian Christians; it literally reads, "The love of Christ holds me together" (2 Cor. 5:14).

What a wonderful and reassuring thought—Jesus Christ is the One who brings every created part together into one wonderful whole. It is Christ who integrates all of life and gives to each of the unique separate parts their meaning, because we only know the meaning of a part of our life as we see its coherence with the whole design.

For example, we can't understand or explain the meaning of an acorn apart from knowing the possibility of the mighty oak tree that it can become. It is only in seeing its potential in comparison to its present state that we can explain an acorn.

The same principle is true when it comes to knowing

people. There is no way I can describe who and what a person is except by a composite that includes the many facts about the past, present, and future of that person: Where did she come from? Who are her family? What are her strong likes and dislikes? What are her crises? What is her destiny? It is Jesus Christ who is able to draw together these individual parts and make sense of them all.

Christ as Head of the Church and Conqueror of Death.

Paul moves now toward the climax of his tribute to Jesus Christ as he writes, "And he is the head of the body, the church: who is the beginning, the firstborn from the dead; that in all things he might have the preeminence" (1:18). It is this same Christ Paul has been describing who created the Church, who gives it meaning and purpose. It is He who guides it toward its eternal destiny. It is Jesus who empowers each of us as individuals and the Church as a whole for the daily task of being His representatives in the world. We eat and work and play and love and worship in the strength and knowledge and wisdom that comes from the Lord.

It is this Jesus, Paul writes, who was the first to conquer death, "The firstborn from the dead." Paul again uses the messianic term "firstborn" to signal Christ's victory over the last enemy—death. It was through the Resurrection that death was conquered and the Church, His new society, was launched.

A Grand Summation.

Paul now concludes this incredible paragraph about Christ by restating his original theme (1:19–20). It is this Jesus who has brought together everything that was estranged. The word "reconcile" in verse 20 is used as a synonym for the word "redemption" that Paul used in verse 14. We learn from this statement that Christ is the Redeemer not only of men and women, but of the entire cosmic order as well, "Things in earth, or things in heaven." This means that the mystery of evil has met its master in the decisive victory won by Jesus Christ, God's beloved Son.

The final words in this paragraph (1:20) tell of the costliness of Christ's reconciling gift, "Through the blood of his cross." The word "blood" is used here in its Old Testament sense of "life given in behalf of another." Jesus Christ has triumphed over death only by His own lonely journey through the valleys of humiliation and death.

The cruelty of crucifixion was the instrument of terror used by the Romans in the first century to maintain control of their empire. But Jesus Christ, by His life, death, and resurrection, disarmed the power of death just as He absorbed the fury that motivates human beings to create such brutal punishments. He brought peace by the sacrifice of Himself, and through His resurrection people of all time have hope for the future.

Paul's portrayal of Jesus Christ in this lesson reveals a new look at the kingly power of God's Son (1:13). His is the power that sets us free (1:14) and forgives sins (1:14). Christ reveals the character of God Himself (1:15); He is Lord over the whole created order (1:16); He has the power of creation (1:16); He has the power to draw together and give meaning to all things (1:17); He is the Lord and Head of the Church (1:18); He has power over death (1:18); and there is no need for further spiritual breakthroughs because the fullness of God's character is in Christ (1:19).

Reconciled through Christ Alone.

Paul, in this early part of his letter to the Christians in Colossae, has stressed in vigorous language the all-sufficiency of Jesus Christ. In addressing the problems that assail the Colossians, he has taken a positive course. He has presented Christ the Savior in living color to a group of Christians who were being distracted by those who denigrated Him.

The best answer then and now to false teaching and false messiahs is the true Messiah. A warm and vital relationship with Christ is the one true answer to all false teaching. Paul urges the Colossian believers to keep their attention focused on Christ. They have already heard and accepted the gospel of the Good News. They have no need for so-called new truth; all they need to do is practice what they have received and remain faithful to it (1:21–23). They must "continue in the faith grounded and settled, and be not moved away from the hope of the gospel" (1:23).

Hope and Glory.

At this point Paul steps back to share with readers something about himself and his motivation. Even though he and his readers have not met personally, Paul wants them to know that they share in his life of faith even as he shares in theirs (1:24–29).

He wants them to see and understand that in spite of the

89

hardship and difficulties he has experienced, his central task is to make the gospel known to the gentile world. Yes, this sharing of the Good News is costly, but Paul affirms that he rejoices in his hardships (1:24).

In verses 26 and 27 Paul mentions the great mystery that stretches back through all the generations of holy history. But now the mystery has been revealed; it "is Christ in you, the hope of glory." The Colossian Christians and non-Jewish believers in Christ anywhere in the world are now, in Christ, at one with God. God so cared for gentile and Jew alike that wholeness in Christ is possible for every person.

Celsus, the second-century cynic and stern critic of Christianity, made a very interesting comment, "The Christians have the absurd idea that God takes an interest in man."

That is just the point; He does!

Father God, You don't just "take an interest in me"—You loved me enough to provide a way for my salvation. I am the apple of Your eye! AMEN.

WHAT THIS SCRIPTURE MEANS TO ME—Colossians 1

"We give thanks to God and the Father of our Lord Jesus Christ, praying always for you" (1:3). This verse reminded me of the time many years ago when I worked as an editorial assistant on one of our denomination's quarterly publications. It was my job to prepare a Missionary Prayer Calendar for each issue. I listed the name of each missionary in the square for his or her birthday date, and our readers prayed for them on their day.

Each month we received letters from missionaries all over the world telling of the added strength they felt on the particular day they were being prayed for. Paul knew all about this, too, for over and over again in his writings he expresses appreciation for the prayers of his friends.

When I read Paul's prayer for his friends to be "fruitful in every good work," I was reminded of an old pear tree that is in an open pasture near our farm in South Texas. Each spring the tree is covered with beautiful white blossoms, then a little later the pears appear. But they're small and hard and full of worms. And it isn't long before they drop to the ground and rot.

The fruit is no good because the tree hasn't been properly cared for in recent years. It hasn't been pruned or sprayed for insects and worms. Good fruit will only grow on a tree that is cared for. In the same way, fruitful Christians can't develop without proper care and nurturing. This comes through fellowship with other Christians, worship and prayer and Bible study. Then, too, we grow as we help others, and as destructive habits are pruned out of our lives.

As a child growing up in the Old South, I pictured Christ as being white, Anglo-Saxon, and having a southern accent. But Paul writes, "By him [Christ] were all things created, that are in heaven, and that are in earth, visible and invisible" (1:16). We understand from these words that He is a cosmic or universal Christ—not a regional or national Savior.

How exciting it is to realize that our Lord is the Creator. He is the One who holds everything together; the One who created Halley's comet and causes it to stay in its orbit and reappear every 76 years. No, I've come to see that my childhood God with a southern accent was far too small.

A later verse in our lesson reminded me of the words in Disney's *Snow White*, "Want to know a secret? Promise not to tell?..." How often as children we've said those very words. Secrets are fun, but they can also be bewildering.

Our son recently took an engineering job with a NASA contractor. One of the first things his employer did was give him several thick manuals that spelled out procedures for company and national security. Secrecy is natural for a children's game and necessary when corporate and national security are at stake.

But Paul gets the message through to us here that our God doesn't deal in secrets. His truth isn't for just a select few. Everyone can know the main secret, "Christ in you, the hope of glory" (1:27). We can know God through Jesus Christ, and Christ can live in us through the Holy Spirit. This grand "mystery" is for everyone!

LESSON 6
COLOSSIANS 2

A Theology of Encouragement

Heavenly Father, Thank You for Your encouragement. You've been there whenever I needed You. Even if I couldn't quite sense Your presence, by faith I accepted Your comfort. Thank You for continuously looking out for me. AMEN.

Paul Expresses Concern. As we have seen in so much of our study, Paul is always intensely interested and emotionally involved in what is happening to his Christian friends across the Roman world. The second section of this letter opens on that note as he writes, "For I would that ye knew what great conflict I have for you, and for them at Laodicea, and for as many as have not seen my face in the flesh" (2:1).

The word translated "conflict" here carries the strong feeling of "struggle"—engaged in a conflict or fight. In fact, the Greek word Paul uses is the root from which our word "agony" comes. In other words, without being overly dramatic, Paul is saying that he is in agony for them. But in this case it doesn't seem that he is undergoing any form of physical or emotional conflict. Rather, the context of the verse suggests that Paul is using this expression here as a synonym for "pray."

Paul is using this descriptive and energetic term to describe his deeply concerned prayer for his readers in Colossae and Laodicea, whom he knows only through the reports from Epaphras and other friends.

While it is obvious from this reference that Paul was deeply disturbed by the introduction of asceticism into these two churches, he always regarded prayer as a highly active and dynamic part of his Christian discipline. Praying, for Paul, meant being engaged in a contest or battle that demanded great concentration and energy.

Since Paul never used words loosely, the force of his feeling here leads us to look more closely at just what was causing him to express such deep concern. From what we have learned already, it is clear that he was greatly alarmed because false teachers had polluted the Colossians' understanding of the gospel as it was first given to them by Epaphras. He knew that the introduction of a false gospel would do great harm to these young churches, and he saw this as an attack by an enemy power that could only be overcome by prayer.

An Encouraging Word.

Then, having made a strong point about the depth of his concern for them, Paul's tone changes a bit. As we've seen again and again in our studies, he is always sensitive to the feelings and needs of his readers. So he now writes that he is praying "that their hearts might be comforted [encouraged], being knit together in love" (2:2).

The word "encourage" is an event word in Paul's mind, as we see here and in his other writings. He knew well the need to be buoyed up and confident in the faith.

At times our Christian walk seems lonely as well as difficult. When we face our problems, the temptation to become discouraged is very strong. We all have those moments when we feel overwhelmed by the complications of family, marriage, children, church life, vocation, and interpersonal relationships. It is then that an encouraging word, not a critical one, can bolster our spirits and give us a new sense of hope.

Earlier we learned that the word Paul uses for "encourage" means literally to "come alongside." So what he is saying in the first part of verse 2 is that they are to be encouraged—they are to come alongside each other—and are bound together in love. Paul wants them to discover the experience of shared love in community. He knows they can handle anything and overcome any obstacle if they are knit together in love. Their quest for truth must rise out of a fellowship in which they express and show love for one another.

Paul, in his typical style, had no intention of soft-pedaling the heresy that had seeped into the church at Colossae. He knew the danger was real, but he also knew that it had to be met with the right spirit. I believe from my own experience in the twentieth-century church that Paul's approach was not only wise but of vital importance for Christians today as we seek to sort out the issues of truth and falsehood.

The dangers of "soft teaching" and false teaching are very real in our churches today. It is important that we stand firm in our knowledge of the faith and not be deluded by a false message in any form. However, there is also the grave danger that in holding to "correct" doctrinal views and biblical interpretations we can become narrow and self-righteous and forget the necessity of Christians' "being alongside each other" in love.

From his words in verse 2 Paul makes it clear that he wants his readers in Colossae to love each other with an encouraging generosity of spirit, while at the same time holding faithfully to the truth with courage and without compromise. In my own experience it is precisely this kind of loving person who is able to be of most help when fellow Christians wander off the doctrinal track. I believe the angry fighters for purity of doctrine have a negative impact because their focus is one-sided and incomplete. Let's face it, angry-looking and angry-sounding Christians are more likely to repel than attract.

The Christian's Legacy.   In this marvelous second verse Paul next tells his readers that they are not only to be encouraged by one another, but also by the "riches" they now have in Jesus Christ. It is estimated that there are thirty-five examples of "wealth words" in the New Testament, most of which show up in Paul's writings. Several of these converge in verse 2 as Paul presses his point that the Colossian Christians are exceedingly rich because of the treasures they have in Christ.

Then, along with the "wealth words," Paul includes some powerful "knowing" words. He wants his readers to know about the vast resource of mystery and knowledge that is their legacy now in Christ Jesus. We see in these words the careful way Paul has been trying to prepare them for their stand against the false teachers mentioned in verse 4.

First, Paul has urged them to discover the resource of love and companionship which they have with one another. He knew that lonely and isolated people are more easily deluded by false promises. Second, he has urged them to recognize the richness they have in the real presence of Jesus Christ.

Paul's approach is very much like that of a good football coach who tries to send his team into a game convinced of two things. First, he wants them to understand that every part of the team—player and coach alike—is important. They all needed each other. Second, he wants everyone to believe that the strategies and plays that have been developed for that game will work. To doubt one or both of these points brings sure defeat.

We can count on God! And we need each other!

Rooted and Alive in Christ.

Before getting down to the nitty gritty of how and what they are to do with and about the false teaching that has invaded their church, Paul gives them these final words (2:4–6). He first warns them about what they are up against—teachers that would beguile or delude them with enticing and persuasive speech. Paul knows how convincing glib arguments can be, and he wants them to clearly understand the danger. This is precisely why Paul wanted them to be fully prepared in every way. They need to have no doubt that their resources in God and each other are adequate to counteract all forms of deceptive and beguiling teaching.

Without that kind of preparation though, we, too, can be easily fooled by half-truths and manipulative arguments. When something sounds good to us, it is dreadfully easy to rationalize non-truth or partial truth into "the truth." Shady and dishonest business decisions have been accepted because of persuasive and glib arguments. And masters of the art of persuasion have convinced whole nations to abandon greater human values in exchange for policies of war and even genocide.

Always the master teacher and a deeply caring human being, Paul understands exactly what his Colossian friends are up against. He knows the challenge that confronts them. Tactfully and thoughtfully he has set out in this remarkable letter to warn them of the dangers they face.

And so Paul concludes these words of preparation for what is to follow with these final instructions: live, abide, in Jesus Christ, "Rooted and built up in him, and stablished in the faith, as ye have been taught, abounding therein with thanksgiving" (2:7). This is the strategy he wants them to remember now. Our strongest defense against all forms of temptation and evil is to be alive in Christ, to be well taught in our faith, and to be thankful, full of gratitude, for God's love and grace.

There's no ring of defeat in Paul's preparation words here. He isn't the least bit grim about the task of living the Christian life. For him, it is a joyous and fulfilling journey of faith. And we catch his mood clearly in this note of thanksgiving. He has done his best to prepare his readers; now he moves ahead boldly.

Look Out! Look to Jesus.

Paul's warning here cannot be misunderstood. The seriousness and gravity of the situation can clearly be seen as he writes "Beware." This is the kind of word a hiker would use to alert a companion to a steep drop-off—"Look out!" It is what we would shout to a friend crossing a busy street who had not seen a speeding car.

What were they to "look out" for? The answer follows immediately. They are to look out "lest any man spoil you" (2:8)—lest anyone carry you away as a captive. Paul quickly explains his meaning. He is warning them not to be carried away by the dangerous content of the false teaching which he now describes.

They are to look out "lest any man spoil you through philosophy and vain deceit, after the tradition of men, after the rudiments of the world, and not after Christ."

It is important to realize that Paul isn't speaking against the love of wisdom, which is what the word philosophy literally means in Greek. He is not denouncing the grand heritage of philosophy in the Greek world of thought. After all, he had earlier quoted with approval the Greek philosophers in his great sermon at Athens (Acts 17).

Instead, Paul is denouncing a kind of philosophy that the Colossians have encountered that is hollow, empty, without content. It is this kind of philosophy that is designed to lead them astray.

Next come some useful clues as to the exact nature of this false teaching that is shaking the church. The King

James text refers to "the rudiments of the world" (2:8). Other translations read, "The elemental spirits of the universe,"—basic worldly principles, the world's crude and unusual ideas. A study of the Greek word that is used here, along with research into ancient Gnostic documents such as the *Book of Enoch* and the *Book of Jubilees*, point toward this explanation. "Rudiments of the world" seems to refer to a kind of theoretical teaching that is fascinated with graduated levels of spiritual reality that flow together to make up the universe.

The whole idea becomes dreadfully complicated because the Greek thinkers of the first and second century

The ruins of the large amphitheater in Hierapolis.

loved to play intellectual games. What evidently was happening, though, is that the Christian gospel was being incorporated into a philosophical framework that made a distinction between "appearance" and "reality." From that point of view the spiritual was "real" and the physical was "appearance." The result of this dichotomy was the practical downgrading of the physical side of existence and the exaltation of the spiritual side of existence.

As I said earlier, this all gets pretty complicated, but the crucial point from the perspective of the Colossian Christians and us is that this line of thought couldn't make any sense at all out of the Jesus Christ who fully identifies with our whole humanity.

This Gnostic perspective would prefer a completely spiritualized Jesus, not the physically real Jesus that the New Testament insists upon. For anyone who took this position, redemption would consist of a liberation from the physical level of existence to the spiritual. And such a view would necessarily downgrade the physical and ethical relationships of everyday existence, since the goal is the gradual upward movement of the spirit of men and women toward higher and higher spiritualization.

Paul, of course, had to expose as false any attempt to transform the Jesus Christ of the gospel into a spirit-redeemer. Such an idea on the part of these false teachers must be denied because it does not allow for the flesh and blood Jesus that we find in the Gospel accounts.

Paul ends verse 8 by bluntly telling his readers that the false philosophy they had been flirting with was "not after [according to] Christ." He is saying here that anyone who had been playing around with this sort of mystery-cult spirit worship has been steadily drifting away from Jesus Christ.

Finally, Paul adds to his grand statement of who Christ is (2:9–10) by saying that "in him dwelleth all the fulness of the Godhead bodily. And ye are complete in him, which is the head of all principality and power." His use of the word "bodily" in verse 9 is to press home the point that God Almighty has spoken through His Son in the flesh—in the real world where we live. Jesus is not a phantom, spiritualized initiator of the spiritualistic—He is Jesus of Nazareth who "came alongside" our lives in the real world of twenty-four-hour days. And it was here in this real world that He won the victory over death and the grave on that first Easter morning.

Paul continues to drive home to his Colossian readers the completeness and all-sufficiency of Christ (2:10). He seems to want to make certain that their attention is focused on Jesus Christ, not as an esthetic spiritual being, but as Jesus who lived and breathed and led a full life telescoped into roughly three years before His very human death and bodily resurrection.

Focus on Christ.

He now reminds his non-Jewish readers that in Christ they have experienced the true circumcision through their baptism (2:11–13). It is possible that Paul opened up the subject of circumcision here because certain of the false teachers may have raised this issue as well. But the circumcision issue had been settled at the Jerusalem Council (Acts 15), and Paul now wishes to assure his readers that they need not be concerned about that kind of legalism. It was true, of course, that circumcision of the male was the sign of the covenant God had made with Abraham, but now that covenant had been fulfilled in Jesus Christ.

Then, too, Paul wanted his readers to understand that it is baptism, not circumcision, that is the present sign of the believer's identification with Jesus Christ. It is also likely that he raised the circumcision issue in order to assure these gentile Christians that in no way were they second-class or incomplete Christians simply because they had not submitted to the Jewish ritual.

Wise pastor and counselor that he was, Paul knew that if the Colossian Christians felt incomplete in any way, they would more easily be trapped by false teaching of either a Jewish or Greek slant. He was fully aware that whether the false ideology tempting these young Christians was a legalistic return to the Law or mystically gnostic, they would be more susceptible if they were feeling inadequate.

On the other hand, Paul wanted to make sure that their focus was on Jesus Christ, for it is in Him that completeness is found and we are forgiven and made alive (2:13). And because of Christ's sacrifice and triumph, "the handwriting of ordinances"—the legal bond that was against us—has been blotted out, cancelled (2:14)! The word translated "handwriting of ordinances" or "bond" was used in the Greek for a promissory note or a written acknowledgement of a debt. In other words, the debt of our sin has been cancelled—"nailed to the cross." In Christ there is complete forgiveness of sins and healing.

As Paul now closes this discussion of the all-sufficiency of Christ, he shows his remarkable mastery of the Greek language by the use of a rare term in verse 15, "And having spoiled principalities and powers" or as some translations read, "He disarmed principalities and powers." The Greek word for "spoiled" or "disarmed" literally means to strip away. Nowhere else in the entire New Testament does this particular term appear, but Paul used it three times in this letter. The picture Paul is giving us is this: Christ has stripped away the very powers of evil.

In this part of our lesson Paul has laid before his readers in Colossae and us two powerful expressions of the significance of Christ's death and resurrection. First, he portrayed Christ as the perfect satisfaction of the Law's demand for justice and righteousness. And second, he pictured the awesome reality of Christ as victor over *all* the forces of evil. All our needs have been met at the cross of Christ!

No One Is Your Judge. Paul now turns his attention to a number of other matters that have apparently been troubling to the Christians in the Colossian church (2:16–19). So often new Christians get sidetracked and lose a clear sense of what deserves to be at the center of their faith. And at such times we find an excessive preoccupation with elaborate details of spirituality and religious forms.

From the list that Paul has included in these verses, it seems clear, as we've already indicated, that the Colossian Christians are troubled by Jewish legalism on one side and Greek spiritualism on the other. He doesn't develop any ranking priority within his list, however.

In verse 16 his list includes practices of Jewish legalism—food and drink laws, holiday and Sabbath observance. But with all of this he concludes that no one should ever be judged by another person on the basis of traditions and ceremonies that are nothing more than "a shadow of things to come" (2:17).

These are indeed liberating words, and they are especially meaningful because they come from a person who had once been strict and narrow during his days as an arrogant Pharisee. He had been guilty of judging others in all of these matters. But in his conversion experience on the Damascus road he had been set free from his confining legalism. He knew full well just how damaging any form of legalism can be as it turns our attention away from Jesus Christ as Savior and Lord.

Then in verses 18 and 19 Paul continues his list by adding the threat from the Greek spiritualistic practices. He warns of the danger of thinking that God is honored by an unhealthy self-abasement, an unwholesome rejection of self as a physical reality. To do this is to reject God's good design in creation in favor of some higher spiritualistic possibility.

But Paul has made it clear to all of his first-century readers and us that our hope does not come in following rules or in observing secret and exotic practices. Rather, it comes to each of us through a living, daily relationship with the Lord.

Christian Freedom.

As Paul prepares now to close out this part of his discussion, he rather bluntly says that if in Christ they had died to the excesses of legalism and to the cultic mysticism of the pagan religions, they have no business now forfeiting their freedom to would-be religious teachers who want to regulate their actions as well as their minds.

And then he concludes with one final observation that is a prime example of Paul's classic wisdom and shrewdness. He points out to his readers that the spiritual exercises and practices of both Jewish legalism and Greek spiritualism have an appearance of wisdom because they promote a rigorous devotion and a severe self-abasement. But in reality, the more such practices are followed, the more attention we pay to that part of ourselves we wanted to bring under control. Or to put it another way, the more we try to suppress our bodies and reject some part of our selfhood—the more we are focused on ourselves—we become obsessed with what we wanted to reject.

But for the Christian there is only one thing to reject—to strip away—and that is sin, with its distrust of God's faithfulness. Instead, some of the Colossian Christians were guilty of rejecting themselves and the concreteness of their existence in favor of rules or self-abasement or exotic practices as a means of heightening their spiritual development. The result, though, of taking this false turn was that they were caught up in elaborate schemes of spiritual development that replaced Jesus Christ as the focus of their attention.

In many ways, the Colossian problem is our problem. We seem to find it so easy in our twentieth-century climate of ingenuity to get caught up with special schemes and programs to promote our own personal growth as well as church growth. We utilize all of the tricks of modern communication and theater to attract people to our denominational homeland and place of worship. We become so busy with methods and programs that we lose sight of the power and attractiveness of Jesus Christ who should be the center of our focus and who alone can meet our deepest needs.

At the same time, we suffer the danger of becoming so preoccupied with spiritual methods and vocabulary that everything else becomes secondary, including our love relationship with Jesus Christ and our fellow Christians.

Paul's counsel to the Colossian Christians is as relevant to us as it was to them, "As ye have therefore received Christ Jesus the Lord, so walk ye in him."

Loving Lord, Help me to walk in You, to walk in repentance, to walk in the Spirit, to live in Your presence—moment by moment. Amen.

WHAT THIS SCRIPTURE MEANS TO ME—Colossians 2

Paul's letter to the Colossians is so warm and personal that I had to be reminded again that he had never visited those three churches in the Lycus Valley, and really didn't know the people he was writing to. But it is true, isn't it, that our lives are often greatly affected by people we've never met.

When I was a child, I had a young playmate who was stricken with polio. I remember so well the anxiety that gripped our family at that time because I had played with my little friend the very week he had taken ill. But my husband and I never had to feel that anxiety and fear when we had our children because of two men we had never met or even seen—Dr. Jonas Salk and Dr. Albert Sabin.

Then as I thought further about this, I realized that all of us owe a heavy debt of gratitude to a great many people we've never met or seen. There are those who preserved the Bible down through the centuries so we can read and study it today. Then there were the inventors of the printing press and the translators who made it possible for me to have my own copy of God's Word, and in a language I can read and understand.

There were those in the history of our country who took a strong stand for religious liberty, making it possible for me to worship in the church of my choice, and those pioneer heroes of the faith who braved all kinds of hardship to build and establish churches. And I owe a great debt of gratitude to countless writers I've never met who have produced books that have blessed and enriched my life.

This is the way it was between Paul and his Colossian friends. By this letter the friends he did not know in person learned from him, and we, too, receive counsel and guidance.

Then as I studied this lesson another powerful truth took on fresh meaning for me. We learned in verses 13 and 14 that not only have our sins been forgiven but the bond that was against us has been cancelled. There are no I.O.U.'s by our name; in Christ we are free from all debt. This truth awakened a vivid childhood memory. When the church I attended in Georgia paid off the debt, the note was burned before the whole congregation. That was an occasion for celebration and joy. What a wonderful picture that gives us—we are debt free in Christ!

There is a third truth in this lesson that has special meaning for me. I'll illustrate it by saying that while I grew up in the Southeast, I have lived much of my adult life in the Southwest. When I first made the change, I was amazed at how the rules about what was right or wrong for a Christian differed. One church enjoyed picnic swimming socials; the other didn't think it was right for men and women to swim in the same pool. One church frowned on playing billiards, another church had billiard tables in their Christian activities building.

Evidently similar differences of opinion on conduct were present in the Colossian congregation, for Paul makes a strong point in this lesson about not judging others by the keeping of certain man-made rules. He didn't want them to get bogged down with petty regulations, but to focus instead on their relationship with Jesus Christ. That was the best behavior regulator then—and it is for us now.

LESSON 7
COLOSSIANS 3—4:1

Life in Christ and Practical Rules for Christian Behavior

Gracious Father, Help me to "seek those things which are above"; to shift my sphere of interest from the things of this world, the dazzling array of things that clamor for more and more of me, but which can never fully satisfy. AMEN.

A Life "Hid with Christ."

Paul continues his Christ-centered teaching (3:1–4) with these opening words, "If ye then be risen with Christ, seek those things which are above, where Christ sitteth on the right hand of God" (3:1). The focus continues to be on Jesus Christ—the center of our faith and the Lord of our lives.

The opening words in verse 1 relate to Paul's earlier reference to his readers being "dead with Christ" (2:20). And here now he writes that "since" you are risen with Christ your lives are to be completely different—"hid with Christ."

Paul has made it clear that the worst kinds of confusion take place if we shift our confidence away from this divine Center of our faith toward other sources, human or "spiritual." And he urges his Colossian readers to fix their minds above such confusion and toward Christ—in whom our lives are hid, in whom we in our sinfulness have died. It is in this same Christ from whom we have received new life, and it is with Christ that we wait for His final appearance (3:3–4).

Paul has emphasized here and his point is clearly made that we are not to look to any other source for the resolution of our past sins or for the infilling of life for our present existence here and now or for the fulfillment of all future hopes and dreams. Jesus is our sufficiency, and because He is, we can pick up on Paul's definition of faith and "put our confidence in the faithfulness of God" as He has made Himself known to us in Christ. His faithfulness is totally adequate for the past, the present, and the future.

To round out the picture, Paul has given us an image of Christ as the center of our faith—he writes that "Christ sitteth on the right hand of God." Here Paul draws on the imagery of Psalm 110:1—a reference that is alluded to many times throughout the New Testament, and for good reason. To the Jews and gentiles of early history the right hand or the right side was considered the place of honor. And so it was quite natural for the early Christian writers, in their effort to picture Christ in all of His glory, to position Him in the place of highest honor, "on the right hand of God."

Here, and in Lessons 5 and 6 (Col. 1 and 2) Paul, as we have seen, has centered the attention of his readers on Jesus. In doing this he has given us the supreme standard for determining whether an interpretation or teaching is false or true.

The reasons why people go adrift and lose touch with the greatest truth and dabble with secondary half-truths are complicated and baffling phenomena that were not only of great concern to Paul in the first century but they are a lively issue in the twentieth century as well. Then and now there were those leaders who for personal reasons—power, ego-satisfaction, popularity, money—attract and influence followers by concentrating on half-truths that offer attractive but false promises. At the same time there may be those in positions of leadership who with sincerity concentrate their teaching on certain partial truths to the exclusion of the whole truth. Such teachers from either side can be most convincing in presenting their points of view.

Let's face it, the young Colossian Christians would have found it very difficult to answer self-assured teachers who urged adherence to the centuries-old collection of Jewish laws and traditions. At the same time it would have been equally difficult to respond to teachers who claimed to have mystical, angelic, or spirit connections. Put in today's idiom, they were "between a rock and a hard place."

Paul knew there was only one answer to their dilemma—and ours. The one true Authority, the Measure by which we can determine truth is Jesus Christ. If a teaching measures up in every way to His love-standard, with all that means, and our lives are "hid with Christ in God," we are prepared as well as we can be to separate that which is false from truth.

Forms of Behavior to Kill—
Put to Death.

We come now to a complete change of tone. Up to this point, Paul has been probing and teaching vital theological truth. Now, as he has done in other letters, he turns to practical matters of Christian behavior—how are we to act in the real world?

Paul opens this section (3:5–11) by writing, "Mortify therefore your members which are upon the earth" (3:5). A literal translation of this makes it a bit easier to understand: "Put to death whatever in your nature is earthy—belongs to the earth." He is referring here to sins toward God and other persons and ourselves. He is not teaching a gnostic rejection of the body or some form of self-abasement. But he does insist that when we experience new life in Christ we are called to the way of discipleship in which we dare to challenge the *tyranny of sin* over our lives. We are to "strip off" harmful and destructive life patterns.

In two lists here, Paul writes of things that must be stripped away. The first he equates with idolatry (3:5), "fornication, uncleanness, inordinate affection, evil concupiscence, and covetousness." All but the last on the list refer to sexual sins. In the first-century pagan world, sexual gratification in or out of marriage was a matter of course. It was not something to be controlled or reserved for marriage, but was to be enjoyed under any and all circumstances. To first-century pagans, the Christian point of view of sex and marriage as given by Jesus was new.

The last on the list, covetousness, implies an insatiable desire for anything—money, power, position, sex. It is quite interesting the way Paul makes the direct connection with idolatry. Paul seems to see these interpersonal sins as directly related to the confusion people have about God—idolatry is the result of the patterns of sinfulness, and sinfulness is the inevitable result of confused worship. Paul uses the word "idolatry" here to convey how people looked to fornication, uncleanness, and the other things on his list, to find help and meaning for their lives. If our worship of God in Christ is pure, the sins in this list will have been "put to death." Our sense of meaning and help for life will come only from God.

Paul then goes on in verses 8 and 9 to list sins that are to be "put off," "anger, wrath, malice, blasphemy, filthy communication" ...lying. The picture we get here may be related to the rite of baptism among the early Christians. Before going into the water they "put off" their old clothes, and then when they came up out of the water, they "put on" new clothes. Here we have the "putting off"; the "putting on" comes shortly.

The Way of Freedom.

The way of freedom in Christian discipleship is another very important teaching that we find in this part of our Scripture lesson. Paul calls upon the Colossian Christians to make vital decisions about the way they live—their pattern of life—decisions only they can make. But he assures them that their resources are readily available through God's faithfulness.

The freedom-in-Christ theme had to be especially helpful to those believers who were being confronted by teachers who were suggesting that Jewish legalism was essential for salvation. This and other forms of legalism restrict the Christian's freedom to be and to grow into the richness of life and experience that God intends for us.

The Promise of Knowledge.

Next, Paul has a word of promise for those Colossian Christians who were being swayed by the secret-knowledge-and-spiritualistic appeal. With marvelous insight he picks up on their "buzz word" when he writes in verse 10 that in Christ believers are being "renewed in *knowledge*." Here they are assured of the wonderful, full, and complete knowledge that God has promised those who choose His way.

The Gospel Is for All.

The final sentence in this particular paragraph (3:11) affirms the universal relevance of the gospel to people of every race and national background. Paul is saying that racism has no part in the nature that has been renewed by the imprint of God's character.

This strong statement on the universality of the gospel is especially interesting in light of conditions in the Colossian church. In these few words Paul speaks directly to the Jewish and non-Jewish circumcision question. And he also takes a swipe at Gnostic arrogance toward the uneducated by his reference to Barbarians and Scythians. To the religiously arrogant Jews (who thought all gentiles were

The ruins of the hotsprings and Roman baths in Hierapolis.

"dogs"), and to the aristocratic and snobbish Greeks, the Barbarians and Scythians were the lowest forms of human life.

In his brief reference to "bond" and "free," Paul undoubtedly added shock to shock as he made the point that in God's sight there is no difference between a slave and a free person. Slaves in the first century had no rights at all, but in God's new society there is no recognition of class. This reference to slavery is also quite significant in view of Paul's letter to Philemon, who lived in or near Colossae, in which Paul made an appeal in behalf of Onesimus, a runaway slave.

In a few words, Paul has let his readers know that in Christ, all the barriers that divide people are down. Christianity is a barrier destroyer—all people are equal before God—Amazing Grace!

We come now to what Paul says the Christian is to "put on" (3:12–14.) As "the elect of God"—chosen people who are holy and loved—they are to be compassionate, kind, humble, gentle, patient, forgiving, and loving.

The Way of Discipleship.

First of all, Paul wanted them to see clearly that they are loved by God, and that His imprint is on their lives. Without that truth firmly fixed in their minds, the rest of what he had to say wouldn't have any particular spiritual significance.

What makes these verses unique are the marks of grace that are scattered at critical places. The paragraph begins with God's prior love as the source for *our* acts of love. We are to forgive because Christ has forgiven us (3:13). Believe me, there is nothing as powerful as Christian forgiveness when a person experiences the gift of truth that "God is for me" (Rom. 8). When we really tap into that spiritual energy source, forgiveness of others becomes a possibility.

Paul builds on all of these marks of grace by saying that the way of love is the bond that integrates all of life (3:14), and he follows up on that by writing, "Let the peace of God rule in your hearts" (3:15). First, it is love that holds everything together, and then the integrative power of love can really work when Christ's healing peace is at work in our lives.

Paul then urges a thankful style of life, and he follows that with this instruction, "Let the word of Christ dwell in you richly in all wisdom" (3:16). He knows full well, and he wants his readers to see too, that our only true Source for power to live effective and worthwhile lives is from Christ and nothing and no one else.

Certainly a mark of this thankful spirit that Paul believes Christians should have is further expressed by his suggestion that his readers should share and sing together from the psalms and hymns and spiritual songs (3:16). And he closes this part of our Scripture lesson by saying that we should "do all [everything] in the name of the Lord Jesus, giving thanks..." (3:17). I am greatly impressed by the joyous and free spirit of exuberance that flows through these verses.

Certainly Paul was keenly aware of the seriousness of the problems that plagued the Colossian church. But he didn't want an oppressive fog or dark cloud of seriousness to rob his readers of the joy of the Lord. I know from my own experience as a pastor in an ideologically intense and spirited university city that one of the good gifts of a Christ-centered faith is a certain lightness that comes from knowing that the Good News is stronger than any other force. We know for sure that it is far stronger than the pessimistic dead-end streets of the cultic movements and the self-centered life-styles of people without God.

I wonder sometimes if we don't take ourselves too seriously and God not seriously enough. Somehow I get the feeling here that Paul wants us to take God seriously and ourselves somewhat more lightly as we share and sing and love with grace in our hearts to the Lord!

Faith at Work in Our Relationships.

The more we study the Apostle Paul—his writings and the man himself—we realize his breadth as a human being. Getting to know Paul just a little is a bit like looking through a kaleidoscope. As we hold this amazing little tube steady, we see a beautiful design in startling colors. Then, as we shift it slightly, the pattern changes as those same particles of colored glass shift into a new position. Another turn of the kaleidoscope, and we see something still different. With each change we may well think we've seen it all. But, no, there's more.

Paul's competence in the theological and biblical understanding of the Christian faith is awesome. His ability to express that understanding in colorful and simple terms has seldom been matched. He is equally at home in an "ivory tower" and in the hurly-burly of city streets. And he is quite comfortable now as he moves into the practical application of his faith to human relationships (3:18–4:1).

In these verses, Paul offers specific counsel to his Colossian readers for their everyday living relationships in the first-century world. In doing this, he continues his customary pattern of relating the separate parts to the greater Center—all relationships are seen through the mediation of Jesus Christ. With Jesus at the center of our lives, all of our relationships with other people are filtered through Him.

Throughout Paul's writings we see that Christ is at the center of all human relationships. In this regard, Paul makes use of a most important phrase—"in the Lord." This phrase appears forty times in Paul's writings but only in one other place in the New Testament (Rev. 14:13). In other words, from Paul's emphasis at the very beginning of this section, we are to see that as he now gets very specific, every relationship we have is "in the Lord." Every part of our lives is to be lived "in the Lord."

Paul begins his specific instructions on relationships with marriage, the most foundational human relationship of all (3:18–19). Here and in Ephesians 5:21–25 we get a sense of mutual submission and love "in the Lord." The will of God, as it is clearly revealed in Jesus Christ, reigns over both husband and wife as they live together in partnership in marriage. There is no contest of will, no jockeying for position and power—both live in love and submission to each other.

This was a revolutionary idea in first-century society. Neither Jewish nor gentile women had any rights in either home or society. Subservience to the husband as master of the home was the accepted pattern. But now, Paul writes that "in the Lord" husband and wife are to submit to each other and love and respect each other. Neither partner is to take the other for granted.

In verse 19, husbands are instructed to love their wives and "be not bitter against them." Other translations of this phrase make it clearer—don't be harsh or hard, be gentle, don't be cross or irritated. So often patience is a lost virtue in the husband-and-wife relationship. Paul wants his Colossian readers to see that their Christianity is meant to work on a day-to-day basis within the home and between wife

Faith at Work between Wives and Husbands.

and husband, with neither one placed at a disadvantage to the other.

Faith at Work between Parents and Children.

Paul now moves on to include the relationship between parents and children as a part of Christian behavior (3:20–21). Children are instructed to obey their parents. The Greek word "obey" in the New Testament is the synonym of the great Hebrew word *shema*, which means "to hear." I think this richer, Old Testament word better expresses the biblical understanding of obedience. This kind of obedience is a dynamic relationship word that has about it the sense of "learning from a teacher."

Paul is urging children to stay in this open and learning position with their parents. And at the same time he has a most important word for fathers, "…provoke not your children to anger, lest they be discouraged" (3:21). This is a much needed and often neglected word. This was also a revolutionary idea in first-century culture where fathers had unquestioned control and mastery over the treatment and even the lives of their children.

But now Paul says that fathers are to be good teachers of their children and exercise Christian love and caring in disciplining them. Children are to be disciplined fairly and without anger. Of course, they need guidance; we all do, but that guidance is to honestly be "in the Lord." Tragically, too many children, even in these enlightened days of the late twentieth century, are unable to "hear" and learn from their parents because mother and father are more undisciplined than the children.

Faith at Work between Servants and Masters.

Paul closes out this relationship section with a rather lengthy discussion of the Christian attitude that is to exist between servants or slaves and their masters (3:22–4:1). This was a major problem in first-century society. The presence of slaves in homes and in the community was not unusual to Paul. But it is possible that his friendship with Onesimus brought this relationship and its problems into sharper focus.

Paul's words to both slaves and masters are carefully surrounded by the checks and balances of the Lordship of Christ. We catch Paul's deep concern that slaves should somehow be able to keep their sanity and feelings of self-worth intact, even though according to Roman law they were nothing but property to their masters.

In the Lord, the Christian slave is to be a better workman, more conscientious, with "singleness of heart, fearing God" (3:22). At the same time, masters are to "give unto your servants that which is *just* and *equal*" (4:1, italics mine). This was the startling Good News that the teachings of Jesus and His followers had for the world of their day.

Paul's counsel to slaves and masters is of great historical interest. It took many centuries for the wicked and inhuman custom of slavery to be abolished from the world. But during those centuries it was Paul's counsel that governed the truly Christian handling of a tragic custom. And while there were those of a "Christian" persuasion who rationalized the validity of slavery, other Christian leaders, such as William Wilberforce, led the fight against it.

At first glance it might seem there is nothing in this section that is relevant to our time, but there is a most practical lesson here for us. The Christian pattern for employees is to faithfully fulfill their work obligation to their employers. And at the same time, employers are to be just and fair in their dealing with employees. Each is to treat the other, not as antagonists who are trying to outdo each other, but as brothers and sisters in Christ.

Our Relationship Responsibility.

But in a larger context, Paul's words to masters have great implications in all of our relationships—between husband and wife, parents and children, friends, employers and employees, and relatives. We are to be "just" and "equal," or "fair," in all of our relationships. The implications, I believe, go far beyond what is legal or custom—we are to be just and fair.

Paul knew that a Christian witness in a relationship of this kind would dispel controversy and false teaching from the Colossian church. He knew that if they would *be* these kinds of witnesses in the Lycus Valley, their message would be powerful and contagious. This was his hope for them—and us!

Almighty God, Help me to be fair and just in my relationships with others. Let Your Lordship, Your love, Your compassion, Your righteousness be evident in every area of my life. Amen.

WHAT THIS SCRIPTURE MEANS TO ME—Colossians 3

When a new semester begins at the seminary where my husband teaches, he usually asks the students in his preaching class to give him some information about themselves. One of the questions he asks is, "Who is your model for preaching?" He says he can usually predict what kinds of sermons they will preach by the answer to that question.

Paul also knew that we become like whatever we admire the most. And for that reason he told his readers then and us now to set our "affections on things above, not on things on the earth." We are to concentrate our full attention on the Lord. He is our model.

I was reminded, too, of some of the things Paul writes about in relation to a popular book entitled *Dress for Success*. The message of this book is that what a person wears has a great deal to do with his or her success in business and society. Usually we can tell a lot about people by the way they dress and how they look.

First, Paul tells us what we are to put off—anger, malice, blasphemy, and so on. Let's face it, these are as out of place for the Christian as wearing tennis shoes with a three-piece suit.

But then he goes on to tell us what we are to put on—compassion, kindness, gentleness, patience, forgiveness, love. It is these that identify the well-dressed Christian just as surely as a well-tailored outfit marks a person with excellent taste.

I like what Paul writes about singing spiritual songs with grace in our hearts. I'm glad the angels aren't the only beings who are able to sing, because I've enjoyed it ever since I learned "I've got the joy, joy, joy down in my heart" in my pre-school days. At college campfires I'd join my friends in singing, "Follow, I would follow thee, my Lord." And when I saw a beautiful sunset, I'd hum, "For the beauty of the earth, for the glory of the skies." At my father's funeral I sang, "The soul that on Jesus hath leaned for repose, I will not, I will not desert to his foes." I was glad for Paul's words here about singing and praising God.

Paul's words about relationships were an important reminder. I'm so thankful for a rich and happy marriage. There's been a lot said on the subject of submission, but I like the way Ruth Graham puts it, "Adjust yourselves to each other out of reverence for Christ." The most critical issue isn't who is "boss," but mutual love and submission in the Lord.

Paul's advice is most helpful as he writes about relationships within the family setting, between employers and employees, and between the Christian and society. I've come to see and understand more clearly than ever before that it is in our relationships with other people that our faith becomes real and alive.

LESSON 8
COLOSSIANS 4

Relationships:
With God and Others

Lord God, Help me to see every relationship as an opportunity to be a blessing. Give me wisdom regarding each one. Teach me how to help bring others closer to You and to do good things for them. AMEN.

Make It Plain.   Paul now moves toward the final words in this important letter with the specific request that the Christians in Colossae pray for him and his friends in Rome. You will remember that he opened this letter by writing that he regularly prays for them (1:3). Now he lets them know of his need for their prayers (4:2–4).

But even in this simply worded request for prayer from his friends, we find, telescoped into a small space, some helpful insights into what it means for us to pray. Paul's first words here are, "Continue in prayer, and watch in the same with thanksgiving" (4:2). As frequently happens, the English translation of this verse, especially in our King James text, doesn't convey the strength and intensity of Paul's meaning.

He uses certain key words that need our attention. First, the word "pray," as we mentioned earlier, means literally to "pray toward." To one versed in Greek, this idea comes through clearly because of the prefix Paul uses with the word "pray." Primarily, prayer, then, has to do with our relationship with God—we "pray toward" Him, we aggressively face toward God. The focus is on God, not on ourselves or what we say—our glibness.

Paul goes on now to write that we are not only to "pray toward" God but that we are to "continue in prayer." Again, the strength of the original is important to our understanding. The thought conveyed here is that we are to persevere in prayer, to be steadfast, to endure, to be doggedly persistent, with our praying. This is the same word Paul used in Romans 12:12, "continuing instant in prayer," and in 1 Thessalonians 5:17, "Pray without ceasing." It bears repeating: For Paul, prayer was hard work; it demanded concentration.

There is no easy way to learn a foreign language or solve a complicated math problem or build lasting relationships. These demand a tenacious "hanging in there" every inch of the way. That's the picture Paul wanted his Colossian readers—and us—to get. From all of this, we see that Paul doesn't treat prayer lightly, as if it were some kind of Christian luxury; instead, it is regarded as a necessity for spiritual health and wholeness.

Another one of Paul's important words in this second verse is "watch." In its oldest form the word means "to wake up from sleep," "to be wide awake," "to be watchful." This is the same word he used in 1 Corinthians 16:13, "Watch ye," in 1 Thessalonians 5:6, "Let us watch," and Luke also used it in Acts 20:31, "Therefore watch"—be alert, be ready.

Prayer is not a vague religious atmosphere of devotion nor is it something to be done dutifully or passively. Rather, it is a careful, wide-awake use of the mind before God. The mind should not be empty or hysterical in prayer, but should be actively thinking through concerns and hopes and reasons for praise as well as petition.

Also found in verse 2 is another characteristic to our praying that is important to Paul: We are to pray "with thanksgiving." Christian prayer has a thread of gratitude running throughout the whole fabric because in Christ we have already discovered His love and faithfulness. This means that our prayers are not persistent directives that distrust the goodwill of the One to whom we pray. But rather there is a persistence that knows of God's love and that He never becomes bored or tired of us.

Paul then in verses 3 and 4 makes two specific prayer requests. First, he asks his readers to join with him in the prayer for open doors—for new and added opportunities "to speak the mystery of Christ" even though he is confined in prison. And, second, he asks them to pray that as a teacher-speaker he will have the ability to make the message of the gospel plain and clear to his listeners. The word for "make it manifest" means to make something visible— make it so clear and plain that it can be seen and felt by his listeners.

It is rather interesting, I think, that Paul used this same word two other times in this letter (1:26 and 3:4). This is undoubtedly not a happenstance. Remember, one of the weightier problems causing confusion in the Lycus Valley churches revolved around the teaching of the mystical Greek spiritualism that placed value on secret understanding and knowledge. Paul, though, wants to make sure his readers understand that the Good News of Jesus Christ is clearly visible to everyone. It is not a mystery known only to a few select initiates—but to everyone!

Wise Conduct and Seasoned Talk.

Paul continues his advice to the young Christians in Colossae with incisive and colorful insight, "Walk in wisdom toward them that are without, redeeming the time. Let your speech be alway with grace, seasoned with salt, that ye may know how ye ought to answer every man" (4:5–6).

The central idea Paul seems to want to get across in verse 5 is that we are to behave wisely and tactfully with those who are not Christians and not a part of the church. The Christian is not to have a holier-than-thou or superior attitude. In our relationships with non-Christians we are to be real and not "otherworldly," otherwise our witness for Christ won't have any meaning to them.

The Greek verb Paul uses here along with the noun *wisdom*, translated "redeeming the time" in our text, actually means to "buy up the opportunity." We are to make the best and wisest use of our time as Christians in our relationship with those around us who aren't believers in Jesus Christ.

I have heard Dr. John Stott, Rector Emeritus of All Souls Church in London, explain Paul's thought this way, "The

Christian church is the only institution in the world that exists for the benefit of those outside of it. This is because the church belongs to a missionary God who has a missionary gospel for a missionary church."

Paul has devoted his life as a Christian to inviting the "outsiders" into the fellowship of believers. He understands how to go about it with directness and tact. There's no thoughtless, bull-in-the-china-shop spirit in Paul's relationship with nonbelievers, and yet he used every opportunity to share with them what the Lord had done for him.

The advice Paul has given us here is extremely vital. Before returning to His Father, Jesus' final instruction was that we are to share our faith with others, no matter where they are. Paul took this command very seriously, and in his wisdom he knew that if we are to be effective in our witnessing we are to be wise and thoughtfully considerate of the feelings of those "outsiders" we want to reach.

Yes, the central focus for our words and actions is Jesus Christ, and He is indeed our model for being and giving a witness to those who are "without." When Jesus was dealing with unchurched nonbelievers, He was the essence of tact and gentleness as He bought up every opportunity to win them. It was only with the self-righteous and arrogant religionists of His day that He was impatient and judgmental.

Few writers have the ability to pack so much into so little. The enormity of truth and just plain good sense that Paul shares in verses 5 and 6 could well be the envy of any author. Now in verse 6, Paul uses two powerful and exciting words to paint the exact picture he wants his readers to see, "Let your speech be alway with *grace*, seasoned with *salt*" (italics mine). The word "grace" (in Greek, *charis*) is a part of Paul's love vocabulary. By the way he uses it, Paul's intended meaning is "surprise love-gift from God." It is "Amazing Grace" that the Apostle invites his Colossian readers to experience and share. But like *agape* love, *charis* love cannot be shared with others until we first receive it ourselves.

The logic of all New Testament ethics is centered in this idea—"We love [God], because he first loved us"; "Let us love one another"; "Grace be unto you, and peace, from God our Father and the Lord Jesus Christ." Biblical behavior is not an ethic based on urgency or guilt or fear—it is rooted in grace. We first experience the surprise gift of love from Jesus Christ, and that motivates us to love and perform loving acts toward those around us.

Briefly, what is conversation that is full of grace? For one thing, I believe Paul felt that Christian conversation should never be dull or boring. We should be good conversationalists who know how to put interesting and exciting words and ideas together. Our conversation should be witty and spontaneous, and full of joy.

In fact, Paul uses a colorful metaphor when he writes that our conversation should be "seasoned with salt," earthy. It should be focused on the things of the Lord, but not loaded down with frivolous jargon that means nothing to "outsiders."

To the first-century person salt was both a preservative and seasoning. I have a feeling that Paul had both of these uses in mind here. Christians are meant to be preservatives in society in witnessing to and living out a gospel of grace day-by-day. And, in addition, the Christian is to give flavor and purpose to life.

Then, based on all of Paul's attitudes, as best we understand them through his writing, I believe these words in verse 6 also convey the idea that we Christians are to live our lives *with style*. It takes style to communicate the Good News of Jesus Christ to teenagers, senior adults, business and professional executives, and to people in another culture. It takes skill, thoughtfulness, and wisdom to witness and live for Christ in a way that is attractive and influences other people. As Christians, this is an art we must study carefully so we are always at our best for the Lord.

Focusing on graceful and well-seasoned conversation will also help keep our priorities in order so that we don't become bogged down with trivialities. And it will help us not to fall for false teaching of any description. Our conversation and speech will be very much "of this world," but its focus will be on Jesus. After all, nonbelievers don't want to get involved in religious arguments or small talk. They not concerned with matters of doctrine. But they can be captivated by the Person of Jesus Christ if we present Him with grace.

There is certainly nothing passive or the least bit careless about the kind of Christian life-style Paul has been setting out for us in these verses. This is not a Sunday religion in which we tip our hats to God once a week if the weather is good. At the same time it is not a several-times-a-week comfortable fellowship with the saints inside of church walls. Instead, we see a vigorous Christian style that calls for us to be keen and sharp, tactful and gentle, alert and learning. In short, it is a demanding but highly rewarding style that gives life the meaning and purpose we long for.

Two Important People in Paul's Life.

Paul's tone changes now as he moves toward the close of this letter. In a sense, he has concluded the advice and counsel part of the letter as he pays tribute to special friends and sends greetings from friends. However, even in these closing words we find some useful words of instructions.

Paul speaks first of Tychicus, "...a beloved brother, and a faithful minister and fellowservant in the Lord" (4:7). Tychicus was from the Roman province of Asia and a good friend of Paul who is also mentioned in Acts 20:4, Ephesians 6:21, 2 Timothy 4:12, and Titus 3:12. Archaeologists have found the name of Tychicus along with the name Onesimus on some inscriptions that were found in the region of Phrygia in Asia Minor.

Tychicus began traveling with Paul on the eastward part of his third missionary journey (Acts 20:4). He was with Paul at Jerusalem, and he was probably a collector for the contributions to those undergoing hardship there (1 Cor. 16:3–4). Tychicus was with Paul in Rome at the time of the writing of this letter, and near the close of Paul's life, around A.D. 67, he was sent by Paul on two final missions (Titus 3:12, 2 Tim. 4:12). Tychicus was likely a person of some importance, and because his home was probably in Ephesus (Eph. 6:21), he was undoubtedly quite familiar with the Lycus Valley churches.

Tychicus' assignment now was to carry this letter from Rome and deliver it to the Christians in Colossae, Hierapolis, and Laodicea—and possibly to Ephesus as well. Accompanying Tychicus on this important mission was "Onesimus, a faithful and beloved brother, who is one of you" (4:9). Onesimus was a common first-century name that meant "useful" and was a name frequently given to slaves.

Most of our information about Onesimus comes from Paul's letter to Philemon, which the two travelers were also carrying with them. Actually, Paul is sending Onesimus, a runaway slave, back to his master, Philemon, who lives in Colossae. But he doesn't refer to Onesimus as a runaway slave, but as a beloved brother. And Paul puts both Tychicus and Onesimus on an equal footing in a very sensitive sentence: "They shall make known unto you all things which are done here."

For Paul, there were no class distinctions in Christ: Both

The piers of a Roman bridge at Laodicea. Laodicea was a textile and medical center in the first century and was located just a few miles south of Hierapolis and a few miles north of Colossae. Because of their proximity the commerce and affairs of all three towns were closely interwoven.

Tychicus and Onesimus were his beloved brothers, both were his friends, both would carry news to the believers in Colossae. Paul's confidence in each man is on the same level.

The Colossian Christians would receive not only this letter, but Paul tells them he is also sending Tychicus and Onesimus to comfort or encourage their hearts (4:8). The word translated "comfort" in our text is the same word we've discussed before, which means "to come along-side." That is precisely what these two men would be doing. They would be "coming alongside" the Colossian Christians to encourage them.

Encouragement from a biblical perspective is very phys-ical and concrete. It is *word* and *work* together—talk and actions. We discover this combination throughout all of Paul's writings. Paul, the great encourager, models for us the pattern for our encouragement of others. It means "something said," because words are the ways we share from mind to mind and mind to heart. We need to hear the words—words of encouragement, of affirmation. But en-couragement must also be a concrete presence—the com-ing alongside of others.

This is a tremendously important message for us in our late-twentieth-century impersonal society. Loneliness pervades our lives even in the crowdedness of a city. Peo-ple all around us are starved for an encouraging word, an expression of affirmation, an arm around the shoulder. Frequently this can be our most effective witness!

Paul now moves on to tell his Colossian readers about other friends of his who send greetings (4:10–17). The en-couragement of Christian friends is always tremendously supportive. When we know that Christians in various parts of the country and even the world are remembering us, it can buoy us and enable us, at times, to achieve some-thing that might otherwise be impossible.

Two names are mentioned in verse 10, Aristarchus and Marcus. Aristarchus was from Thessalonica, the capital city of the Roman province of Macedonia. We don't know a great deal about him, but like Tychicus he had traveled with Paul from Jerusalem to Rome. In addition to being mentioned in this Colossian letter, there are also refer-ences to him in Acts 20:4 and 27:2, and Philemon 24. It is

Special Greetings from Special Friends.

possible also that this is the same Aristarchus who is mentioned in Acts 19:29 and was in the middle of that mob scene in Ephesus.

The second name in verse 10 is Marcus. This is the John Mark who had accompanied Paul and Barnabas partway on their first missionary journey about twelve years before. You will recall that Paul and Barnabas split up at the beginning of the second missionary journey because of Mark. He had deserted the party partway through the first trip. Apparently that rift had been healed because Mark was with Paul in Rome. Further mention is made of Mark in the letter to Philemon and 2 Timothy. And it is this Mark who is credited with the Gospel that bears his name.

Of "Jesus, which is called Justus" (4:11) we know nothing except that he was a Jewish Christian who was with Paul. Epaphras has been mentioned before. He was well known to Paul's readers because he had been—or was—a minister to the Colossian church. He also served as "senior pastor," to use a contemporary term, to the churches in all three Lycus Valley towns—Colossae, Hierapolis, and Laodicea.

In verse 14, Luke's name is added to the list. Luke, "the beloved physician," had traveled extensively with Paul. As the author of both the Gospel that bears his name and the Book of Acts, Luke's name is most familiar to us. The second name mentioned in verse 14 is Demas. Little is known of this man except that he was a fellow laborer with Paul and later deserted Paul "...having loved this present world" (2 Tim. 4:10).

Greetings are sent in verse 15 to Nymphas in whose house the church at Laodicea met. In our King James text, Nymphas seems to be a man, but in other translations the reference is to Nympha "and the church in her house." This was a first-century house church because there were no formalized church buildings that early in Christian history. This same kind of reference was made to Prisca and Aquila in Paul's letter to the Romans where he greeted them and the church in their house, and a similar reference turns up in Philemon 2.

Assuming the greater accuracy of later translations and that Nympha was a woman leader in the Laodicean church only further emphasizes the importance of women in the early church. You will recall that Paul's first convert in Europe was Lydia in Philippi and that the church there first met in her home (Acts 16). Then in Acts 17, reference is made to leading women in the church at Thessalonica, and later in this same chapter, a woman named Damaris is mentioned in connection with the church in Athens. Priscilla was a spiritual leader in the Corinthian church, and Euodias and Syntyche were both prominent in the church at Philippi.

Women were key participants during the ministry of Jesus as well. The first preacher of the Good News to non-Jews was the woman at the well, who proclaimed Jesus as the Messiah to her townspeople (John 4). The first preachers of the Resurrection were the women who first discovered the empty tomb and were told to go and tell the disciples.

Even though women were generally restricted in the Mediterranean world of the first century, in the church they held positions of leadership in accordance with the gifts the Holy Spirit had given them. The prominence of women in the life and ministry of the church has continued since the time of the New Testament, but not without periods of setback and resistance. But the fact remains—the barriers were broken down in Christ. Women, past and present, were and are gifted by the Holy Spirit for positions of leadership.

The final name in Paul's list is Archippus (4:17). He is mentioned only here and in Philemon 2. He lived in either Colossae or Laodicea, and Paul now asks that his readers join him in urging Archippus to fulfill the ministry he has received from the Lord. We have no idea what the distraction was. Knowing that people then weren't all that different from people now, it may be that Archippus was suffering from feelings of inadequacy. But whatever it was, Paul urges him to find his place of service—"to get his act together"—and move ahead with the Lord's work.

Throughout all of Paul's writings we find him encouraging Christians to find their places of service and become active in them. And whatever the crisis that was confronting Archippus, the mention of Paul's interest must have been a challenge to him to get on with the important work that was his.

Paul has not given cheap advice in this letter. Instead, he has pointed his first-century readers and us toward the living Center of our faith—Jesus Christ. From that foundation, he has taught the healthy doctrine of Christian discipleship and Christian freedom that sets up the right balance between our trust in God's faithfulness and our need to make our own decisions. We see this now in his mention of Archippus. Paul doesn't scold him or tell him what to do. Instead he respects and trusts his wavering friend in the Lord.

Nowhere in this letter do we see an authoritarian or patronizing Paul. His respect for the personhood of his readers gives us a keen model for our own discipleship. Paul never gives us the impression that "he has arrived." Instead, we read him as a fellow traveler who is on the pilgrimage with us.

A Last Word. Up to this point, a secretary has taken down Paul's words in the very tight Greek lettering that was traditional of first-century letters. Now, Paul takes the writing instrument from the secretary and adds his final words, "Remember my bonds. Grace be with you" (4:18). This word of grace comes from the heart of Paul to his readers of all time.

We have seen in our study of both Philippians and Colossians that Paul had no shortage of ego strength; he never hesitated to tell his readers about himself and his life. At times I've heard readers of Paul, who may be reading him superficially, express offense over his frequent references to himself. But it has been my experience both in life and in reading that the best writers and the healthiest people let others know who they are and what they think. Paul was always frank about his feelings, sensitive to the concerns of others, vulnerable and open.

The more I've studied this great Apostle, the more I like him, and the more I learn from him. It isn't surprising to me that he and Seneca and Suetonius had stimulating conversations in Rome. I'm thankful that he and Peter, the great fisherman, confronted their differences head-on and came up with the right answers. I like the strong-willed Paul who was unrelenting in his judgment of young John Mark, but went on later to discover in a more mature Mark a beloved friend and Christian brother. For me, Paul is the classic nonhero who wrote weighty letters but probably wasn't all that impressive looking in person. Yet he was a man who kept his friends and loved his enemies, and most important of all, he kept the faith.

Dear Father, Teach me to persevere in prayer—to be steadfast, "doggedly persistent," to refuse to let go of You, to remain prayerful and aware of your presence throughout the day. AMEN.

WHAT THIS SCRIPTURE MEANS TO ME—Colossians 4

I was invited to a meeting of a woman's group to hear an expert talk on time management. That is a subject that interests me because I never seem to have enough time to get everything done.

The speaker said that managing time was a matter of setting priorities and then implementing them. I suspect that is what Paul was thinking about when he counseled his readers with these words, "Walk in wisdom toward them that are without, redeeming the time" (4:5). Or, he might have worded it this way, "Live wisely before non-Christians and take full advantage of every opportunity."

I realize that sometimes I fret about lack of time when in reality I'm not really making the best use of the time and opportunities that God has given me. And at the same time I know that the way I choose to use my hours and days says a great deal to other people about what is important to me.

When I was going to visit our children in another city at Thanksgiving, a friend said, "Would you please call our daughter-in-law and tell her you've seen us? It would mean a great deal to her to have some direct word from us." I was reminded of that request when I read in our lesson about Paul asking Tychicus and Onesimus to bring the Colossian Christians up-to-date on all that was happening with him. Then, as now, keeping in touch was important. Newsy letters of encouragement can mean so much to our relatives and friends.

Paul was always very sensitive to the importance of relationships. And in this last chapter of Colossians he mentions a number of people. Mark and Luke, of course, are credited with writing three of our New Testament books. Both men were important to Paul. I'm sure he had a special feeling for Mark because of their renewed relationship after the serious rift that was caused by Mark's desertion during Paul's second missionary journey. It is this renewed relationship that reminds me of the importance of keeping an open and generous mind toward other people.

Throughout all of his Christian life Paul seemed to draw great strength from his friends. Christianity is never a "Lone Ranger" affair. We need each other, and we especially need the trust and support of Christian friends. That is one reason why being active in the fellowship of a church group contributes so much to our own walk with the Lord. It is there that we not only receive the support of others, but we are able to give support.

At the very end of the letter Paul makes a final appeal, "Remember my bonds." This reminds me of just how fortunate we are to live in a country where we have religious freedom. Paul was in prison simply because his loyalty to the Lord who met him on the Damascus road went counter to the worship of the Roman emperor.

At the same time I am reminded that there are places even in our twentieth-century world where Christians cannot worship in freedom, and where some are in prison for their faith in Christ. The lesson for me here is to remember to pray for them even as Paul asked his Colossian readers to pray for him.